I0438954

Use of Multidimensional Modeling to Evaluate a Channel Restoration Design for the Kootenai River, Idaho

By B.L. Logan, R.R. McDonald, J.M. Nelson, P.J. Kinzel, and G.J. Barton

Prepared in cooperation with the Kootenai Tribe of Idaho and Bonneville Power Administration

Scientific Investigations Report 2010–5213

U.S. Department of the Interior
U.S. Geological Survey

U.S. Department of the Interior
KEN SALAZAR, Secretary

U.S. Geological Survey
Marcia K. McNutt, Director

U.S. Geological Survey, Reston, Virginia: 2011

For more information on the USGS—the Federal source for science about the Earth, its natural and living resources, natural hazards, and the environment, visit http://www.usgs.gov or call 1-888-ASK-USGS

For an overview of USGS information products, including maps, imagery, and publications, visit http://www.usgs.gov/pubprod

To order this and other USGS information products, visit http://store.usgs.gov

Contents

Figures

Tables

Conversion Factors

Multiply	By	To obtain
centimeter (cm)	0.3937	inch (in.)
cubic meter per second (m³/s)	70.07	acre-foot per day
cubic meter per second (m³/s)	35.31	cubic foot per second (ft³/s)
kilometer (km)	0.6214	mile (mi)
liter per second (L/s)	15.85	gallon per minute
meter (m)	3.281	foot (ft)
meter per second (m/s)	3.281	foot per second (ft/s)
newton per square meter (N/m²)	10	dyne per square centimeter (dyn/cm²)
square meter (m²)	0.0002471	acre
square meter per second (m²/s)	10,000	stoke

Vertical coordinate information is referenced to the North American Vertical Datum of 1988 (NAVD 88).

Horizontal coordinate information is referenced to the North American Datum of 1983 and Idaho Transverse Mercator – North American Datum 1983/1998 Idaho West, in meters.

Abbreviations and Acronyms

AEP	annual exceedance probability
D_{50}	median grain-size diameter
FaSTMECH	Flow and Sediment Transport with Morphologic Evolution of Channels
HSC	habitat suitability criteria
GPS	global positioning system
LIDAR	light detection and ranging
MD_SWMS	Multidimensional Surface-Water Modeling System
MSL	modeled spawning locations
RKM	river kilometers
RMS	root-mean square
WUA	weighted usable area

Use of Multidimensional Modeling to Evaluate a Channel Restoration Design for the Kootenai River, Idaho

By B.L. Logan, R.R. McDonald, J.M. Nelson, P.J. Kinzel, and G.J. Barton

Abstract

River channel construction projects aimed at restoring or improving degraded waterways have become common but have been variously successful. In this report a methodology is proposed to evaluate channel designs before channels are built by using multidimensional modeling and analysis. This approach allows detailed analysis of water-surface profiles, sediment transport, and aquatic habitat that may result if the design is implemented. The method presented here addresses the need to model a range of potential stream-discharge and channel-roughness conditions to best assess the function of the design channel for a suite of possible conditions. This methodology is demonstrated by using a preliminary channel-restoration design proposed for a part of the Kootenai River in northern Idaho designated as critical habitat for the endangered white sturgeon (*Acipenser transmontanus*) and evaluating the design on the basis of simulations with the Flow and Sediment Transport with Morphologic Evolution of Channels (FaSTMECH) model. This evaluation indicated substantial problems with the preliminary design because boundary conditions used in the design were inconsistent with best estimates of future conditions. As a result, simulated water-surface levels did not meet target levels that corresponded to the designed bankfull surfaces; therefore, the flood plain would not function as intended. Sediment-transport analyses indicated that both the current channel of the Kootenai River and the design channel are largely unable to move the bed material through the reach at bankfull discharge. Therefore, sediment delivered to the design channel would likely be deposited within the reach instead of passing through it as planned. Consequently, the design channel geometry would adjust through time. Despite these issues, the design channel would provide more aquatic habitat suitable for spawning white sturgeon (*Acipenser transmontanus*) at lower discharges than is currently available in the Kootenai River. The evaluation methodology identified potential problems with the design channel that can be addressed through design modifications to better meet project objectives before channel construction.

Introduction

Channel construction projects designed to restore degraded waterways have become a common practice nationwide. Restoring dynamic river processes that help create and maintain self-sustaining ecosystems (Wohl and others, 2005) remains challenging because the complex interactions between water and sediment that determine river morphology are difficult to predict. The relative immaturity of the field of restoration and shortcomings in existing methodologies for evaluating channel designs contribute to this problem, leading to project failures (Babcock, 1986; Frissell and Nawa, 1992; Kondolf and others, 2001; Tompkins and Kondolf, 2007). The call for increased monitoring of constructed channels to learn which techniques do and do not work is ubiquitous (Kondolf and Micheli, 1995; Palmer and others, 2005; Shields and others, 2003; Moerke and Lamberti, 2004; Rosgen, 1996) and may lead to improved channel restoration projects.

An alternative approach is to detect project flaws before the channels are built by using numerical models to simulate hydraulic and sediment-transport processes in the proposed channel. Although some channel designs are developed in part through the use of one-dimensional models, others are designed by scaling channel characteristics on the basis of reference reaches or through the use of other empirical relations (Hey, 2006). Consequently, many channel restoration projects are constructed without the aid of modeling to help predict streamflow characteristics important for channel function and stability.

Multidimensional models (two- and three-dimensional models) can provide detailed estimates of hydraulic conditions that cannot be simulated in one-dimensional models. Although one-dimensional models require less input data and are computationally fast, they only provide at-a-section or reach-averaged analyses, which means simulated output such as stream depth and velocity are averaged over a cross section or reach. Multidimensional models provide information about the spatial distribution of the water surface, stream depth, stream velocity, and shear stress throughout the modeled channel. This information can be used in many different ways; for example, to determine whether the proposed channel can convey potential streamflows at all points in the channel rather than only at selected cross sections; to identify localized areas where stress may be unexpectedly high, which could lead to local erosion; or to assess prospective aquatic habitat at ecologically meaningful scales in the channel. The spatial distribution of shear stress is also necessary to accurately predict sediment transport. In addition, multidimensional models can simulate the hydraulic processes related to backwatering and the development of recirculating zones or eddies. These models are also capable of simulating lateral differences in water-surface elevation such as super elevation of the water-surface profile in the outside of river bends. Multidimensional models are better suited to represent complex channel designs because, unlike one-dimensional models, multidimensional models can incorporate potential changes to channel alignment or restoration structures that redirect flow, such as j-hooks, groins, and weirs (Rosgen, 1996) explicitly in the model topography. Thus, multidimensional models provide more detailed results and more accurate simulation of many river processes than one-dimensional models.

To address the need for evaluation of channel restoration designs, the U.S. Geological Survey (USGS), in cooperation with the Kootenai Tribe of Idaho and Bonneville Power Administration, investigated a methodology to assess channel designs using a multidimensional hydraulic model. In this report a methodology is proposed to evaluate key aspects of channel function by focusing on potential (1) water-surface levels, (2) sediment transport, and (3) aquatic habitat characteristics. Water-surface levels are assessed to ensure that water-surface profiles match the design-channel morphology so that flood-plain connectivity as well as flood-conveyance needs are met. Sediment transport is evaluated in terms of potential sediment mobility and transport mode as indications of channel stability. The aquatic habitat created by the design channel is assessed by using criteria established for target species of interest to evaluate the amount and quality of aquatic habitat. All three aspects of channel function are evaluated for an appropriate range of discharge and sediment conditions in order to characterize the channel response to a suite of potential conditions.

The proposed methodology is demonstrated by applying it to a preliminary channel design, which was developed in part through the use of one-dimensional models, proposed to enhance aquatic habitat for the endangered Kootenai River white sturgeon (*Acipenser transmontanus*) in the Kootenai River in northern Idaho. The existing Kootenai River also was modeled for the same suite of streamflow conditions. The same evaluation techniques were applied to the existing Kootenai River, which is referred to in this report as the Kootenai River, and to the preliminary design, which is referred to as the design channel, to learn how each channel functions, or would function, and to make comparisons between the two channels.

The purpose of this report is to describe a methodology for using multidimensional modeling to evaluate channel restoration designs before the channels are constructed. This methodology is demonstrated using a proposed channel restoration for a 14.3-km reach of the Kootenai River in Idaho. The design evaluation methodology includes selection of an appropriate range of streamflow conditions and hydraulic roughness values to use in multidimensional modeling. The methodology then involves the use of modeling results to evaluate water-surface levels, sediment transport, and aquatic habitat for design channels. The report describes the development and specifications of the Kootenai River channel design, the strategy and methodology of the streamflow modeling used to evaluate the design, the modeling results and potential implications, and considerations for additional analyses.

Use of Multidimensional Modeling to Evaluate Channel Restoration Designs

There are two essential steps in using multidimensional models to evaluate channel restoration designs before the channels are constructed. First, critical decisions about the modeling application needs to be made, including identifying the stream discharges to be used in analyzing the stability and function of the design and determining the appropriate roughness values for the modeling, both of which are essential for producing reasonable and reliable results. Second, model results are analyzed to understand how the design channel will potentially function in terms of water-surface levels, sediment transport, and aquatic habitat. This two-part approach helps in understanding how the design channel will function for a range of conditions and in identifying potential issues that may arise if the streamflow conditions or roughness are different from those anticipated.

Modeling Considerations

Selecting Discharge

Careful selection of the modeled discharges will help ensure that the design channel will function as expected. At a minimum, model simulations and analysis need to be based on two discharges. The first is the design discharge that was used to determine the principal design channel morphology; the second is a much higher, relatively rare discharge that enables an assessment of potential flood conditions. The design discharge typically is the estimated bankfull discharge, commonly considered the flow that shapes channel geometry and defines and maintains the flood plain (Wolman and Miller, 1960; Copeland and others, 2001). However, the effective discharge and discharges that correspond to given return-interval discharges may be more indicative of the channel-forming discharge than the design discharge (Shields and others, 2003; Doyle and others, 2007) and need to be considered for modeling if they differ substantially from the design discharge. Modeling the design discharge helps assess whether or not the design channel will function as planned at the intended discharge. If the channel will not function as planned, the design will need to be modified. It is also important to model a higher discharge, which may be the 1-percent annual exceedance probability (AEP) flood discharge (also known as the 100-year flood) or other discharge, depending on the degree of acceptable risk, to assess potential flooding and the ability of the design to sustain more extreme conditions (Smith and Prestegaard, 2005).

Ideally, a series of discharge values is modeled to provide more complete information about channel function through the likely range of streamflow conditions. Discharges both higher and lower than the design discharge may cause substantial geomorphic changes. For example, two reconfigured streams in Colorado changed considerably following flows comparable to the 16.7-percent and 25-percent AEP floods (Elliott and Capesius, 2009). These flows were only slightly larger than the bankfull discharge, which is commonly reported to be the 50-percent AEP flood. Flows that are less than bankfull may alter the channel by eroding and depositing fine sediment, such as sand and silt, in localized areas (Smith and Prestegaard, 2005). Evaluating a range of discharges may also provide insight about channel habitat available for specific life-stages of fish, such as adults during spawning discharges or development and transport of fry during lower discharges. Additionally, if certain ranges of discharge are perceived as critical because of habitat considerations, these discharges need to be included in the range of modeled discharges.

Selecting Hydraulic Roughness

The hydraulic roughness of a river channel is an important control on flow characteristics and is difficult to estimate or predict. Sources of roughness in a river channel include the alignment of the channel banks, bank irregularities, bed material, bedforms, and vegetation. Because it is difficult to quantify the contributions of various sources of roughness, it is common to group all sources of roughness into a single parameter, such as Manning's n or a drag coefficient, for modeling purposes.

In modeling applications, the total roughness value is typically determined in one of two ways. First, streamflow models can be calibrated by adjusting the roughness parameter until the resulting water-surface profile matches field surveys of the water-surface profile at a known discharge. Second, roughness can be specified by using empirical data for sediment grain size, bedform geometry, and bank roughness.

Unfortunately, models for design channels cannot be calibrated by adjusting the roughness parameter because water-surface profile data are not available. Detailed information about bed grain sizes and bedforms is also unavailable. This

makes selecting appropriate roughness values for a proposed channel a challenging aspect of design-channel evaluation.

Although models for design channels cannot be calibrated in the traditional sense, selecting reasonably appropriate roughness values for modeling streamflow in design channels can be accomplished by using one of three methods. First, roughness values determined for the unaltered channel can be applied directly to the design channel for the same or similar reach. This method may be appropriate if there are only moderate planned changes to channel alignment, bank roughness, and bed material so that the average channel roughness remains largely the same. Second, the roughness of the design channel can be adjusted in the model until the predicted water-surface profile matches the water-surface profile measured in the unaltered reach. This assumes that the roughness will adjust to give the same head loss through the reach before and after restoration. This method may be appropriate in short reaches with negligible expected change in water-surface slope, even if there are more substantial planned changes to channel alignment, bank roughness, and(or) bed material. Finally, the design-channel roughness can be specified by the designer explicitly, such as by assigning a Manning's n value, or may be calibrated on the basis of water-surface profiles developed through modeling. This last method heavily relies on the designer's professional experience and the designer's estimate of the roughness of the finished channel but may be the only option if substantial channel change is proposed over long reaches of the river. For all three methods, the roughness values used need to be reasonable and feasible given what is known about the present system and the proposed changes to the channel.

Because of the uncertainty in estimating roughness for a design channel, sensitivity analyses of the design model are performed by using different roughness values in model simulations. In general, roughness values larger and smaller than the primary roughness values used in the modeling are evaluated on the basis of simulation results. In some cases, selecting the range of roughness values can be guided by the range of values calibrated for different discharges in the unaltered channel. For the work on the Kootenai River described in this report roughness values were modeled that were 50 percent and 200 percent of the primary drag coefficients selected. The basis for varying other roughness parameters, such as z_0 (boundary roughness length), Chezy coefficients, or Manning's n, however, would require more reasoning because each parameter is defined differently. The range of realistic roughness values will also vary among river channels and need to be evaluated on a case-by-case basis.

Channel Evaluation Techniques

Water-Surface Levels

Analysis of the water-surface levels helps ensure that the levels match the channel morphology, which is important for assessing flood-plain connection and function as well as flood potential. Examining water levels early in the design process will identify first-order problems in the routing of water through the design channel that need to be corrected before more extensive analysis and modeling work is performed. If the design discharge is based on the bankfull discharge, then on average the water surface at bankfull discharge will just reach the flood plain without overtopping the channel bank (Copeland and others, 2001). If the modeled water surface is too low, the flood plain may not be inundated frequently enough to maintain riparian vegetation and wetland conditions. If the modeled water surface is too high, the flood plain may be inundated more frequently at greater depths, which could remove or kill riparian vegetation. Channel designs also need to be checked to ensure that the channel is capable of conveying the target high discharge without flooding.

Sediment Transport

Sediment transport is evaluated to provide an indication of channel stability. A stable river channel, whether natural or constructed, implies there is a balance between the incoming and outgoing sediment load. However, alluvial rivers can be stable yet continue to migrate provided that channel width, slope, depth, and sediment input and output remain unchanged in the long term (Shields and others, 2003). Conveying the appropriate amount of sediment is therefore critical to maintaining the stability of channels designed with fixed banks that are not allowed to adjust through time. Sediment transport can be assessed by using a multidimensional model to predict sediment mobility and transport mode for a range of discharges.

Sediment mobility is important to channel stability because if the sediment is supplied from upstream but becomes immobile in the design reach, it will be deposited in the design reach. On the other hand, if sediment of a given size is present and readily moved in the design reach but supplied at a relatively low rate from upstream, erosion may occur. In general, most channels need to be capable of moving the median grain size either at the bankfull discharge or the effective discharge. Mobility can be evaluated by determining whether the stress acting on the channel bed is sufficient to move the sediment. To do this, for this study equations from Parker and others (2003) were used to determine the dimensionless shear stress required to produce true initial motion of the D_{50} bed material (material having the median, or 50th-percentile, grain-size diameter) for the reach. In other systems it may be more important to evaluate sediment transport in terms of significant motion, in which much of the bed sediment is mobile.

The transport mode of the sediment in the reach also has an important function in processes that govern channel stability. The transport mode of finer-grained sediment were evaluated by using the Rouse number, which determines whether sediment will move fully in suspension, partially suspended, or as bedload (Rouse, 1937). The Rouse number is the ratio of the particle settling velocity to the strength of the turbulence, and is calculated as

$$Rouse\,number = \frac{w_s}{\kappa u_*},\qquad (1)$$

where κ is Von Karman's coefficient (typically 0.4), w_s is the particle settling velocity, and u_* is the shear velocity defined by $u_* = \sqrt{\tau_b/\rho}$, when τ_b is bottom stress and ρ is the density of water. For Rouse numbers greater than or equal to 2.5, the ratio w_s to κu_* is 1 or less and the particle is unlikely to be suspended (Middleton and Southard, 1984). Therefore, Rouse numbers greater than or equal to 2.5 indicate that the sand will move primarily as bedload. For this report, Rouse numbers less than 2.5 are divided into the following categories: 1.2 to 2.5, indicating that some portion of the sand moves as suspended material; 0.8 to 1.2, indicating that the majority of sand moves in suspension; and less than 0.8, indicating that virtually all sand is in suspension and that there is little variation in sediment concentration in the vertical.

Aquatic Habitat

Channels designed primarily to restore or enhance aquatic habitat for fish and other species can be evaluated to determine the quantity and quality of aquatic habitat created. This is accomplished by using aquatic habitat suitability criteria (HSC), which assign values of suitability to hydraulic and(or) physical characteristics, such as depth, velocity, substrate, and cover, for target species and life stages. HSC can be binary functions, in which an observed characteristic is assigned a value of 0 (unsuitable) or 1 (suitable), or can be univariate, in which suitability values of 0 to 1 are assigned to a range of depths, velocities, or substrate sizes (Waddle, 2001). This methodology uses the results from hydraulic model simulations to assign a suitability value for each aquatic habitat characteristic at each cell in the model computational grid. The composite suitability of each cell is determined by using the mean or geometric mean of all aquatic habitat characteristics. This information can be further summarized by calculating the weighted usable area (WUA), which has units of square meters (m^2), by multiplying the area of each cell by the composite suitability of the cell and summing over the area modeled. The WUA can be calculated for each discharge modeled to show the relation between available aquatic habitat and discharge.

Evaluation of a Channel Restoration Design for the Kootenai River

The methodology described herein was applied to a preliminary channel design proposed to improve aquatic habitat in the Kootenai River for white sturgeon. This example illustrates the process of selecting streamflow conditions and the difficulties associated with selecting appropriate roughness values to model design channels. The process of evaluating the design channel is carried out by examining the modeled water-surface levels, sediment-transport indicators, and aquatic habitat potentially available in the design.

Project Background

The Kootenai River flows south out of British Columbia, Canada, through Montana and Idaho, and then flows northwest back into British Columbia. The study reach, located near Bonners Ferry, Idaho, contains a marked transition between a relatively steep canyon reach with an average annual discharge of 387.3 m³/s (at the U.S. Geological Survey streamgaging station Kootenai River at Leonia, station 12305000) to an extremely low gradient lacustrine valley that ends at Kootenay Lake (spelled Kootenay for Canadian waters; figs. 1 and 2). This sharp slope change results in deposition of the coarse fraction of the sediment load, which produces a quasi-braided gravel reach that transitions to a low-gradient meander reach. The median grain size diameter (D_{50}) in the braided reach is 3.4 cm. The bed-material size decreases in the downstream direction to the meander reach, which is dominated by fine sand with a D_{50} of 0.023 cm. The slope through this transition decreases by an order of magnitude, from 0.00046 near the top of the braided reach to 0.00002 in the meander reach.

Flow and sediment transport in the lower Kootenai River are strongly influenced by the water level of Kootenay Lake, located more than 100 river kilometers (RKMs) downstream from the reach modeled in this study. Kootenay Lake levels have fluctuated from 532 m to 535 m above the North American Vertical Datum of 1988 since completion of Libby Dam upstream. The low valley slope of the Kootenai River through the meander reach allows Kootenay Lake to cause backwater conditions to varying degrees in the study area. The backwater can extend upstream as far as RKM 247.5 to RKM 257 (Berenbrock, 2006); the location changes in response to seasonal variations in river discharge and levels in Kootenay Lake (Berenbrock and Bennett, 2005). When the backwater extends farther upstream, the water-surface slope flattens, which reduces sediment transport.

The study area contains a portion of the 29.5-km reach designated as critical aquatic habitat (RKM 257 to RKM 228) for the Kootenai River white sturgeon (*Acipenser transmontanus*), which was listed as an endangered species in 1994 (U.S. Fish and Wildlife Service, 1994, 2006, 2008). Young white sturgeons have not successfully survived to form an age class capable of sustaining the population since 1974 (Paragamian and others, 2005). This problem, known as recruitment failure, occurs between the embryo and larval stages (U.S. Fish and Wildlife Service, 1999). Lack of recruitment success has been attributed at least in part to alteration of the natural flow regime since completion of Libby Dam in 1972. Full flow regulation, which began in 1974, substantially altered flow patterns, reduced the peak flow by nearly half, increased base flow, and altered the sediment regime. Other anthropogenic

changes to the Kootenai River include construction of dikes on natural levees, changes to the level of Kootenay Lake that alter the extent of backwater, loss of wetlands, reduction in nutrient load, and fishing (Barton and others 2005).

Many different hypotheses have been advanced to explain the cause of recruitment failure (see Kootenai Tribe of Idaho, 2009, for a more detailed summary). One class of hypotheses indicates that the sturgeon always spawned in the meander reach, but that the meander reach has become unsuitable because of the presence of sand which may suffocate sturgeon eggs and otherwise be detrimental to the fish. The presence of sand has been attributed to invasion of sand caused by post-dam hydraulics and erosion or to a lack of peak flows capable of scouring sand from the reach. A second class of recruitment hypotheses proposes that sturgeon previously spawned farther upstream but no longer are able to reach former spawning locations. The failure to spawn farther upstream has been attributed to various issues including incorrect imprinting locations, incorrect homing locations, shifted hydraulic or bio-logical spawning cues, or migration barriers. Other hypotheses indicate that large-scale ecosystem degradation, loss of ripar-ian habitat, altered flow regime, or lack of sufficient remaining broodstock may be a cause of recruitment failure.

In 2006, a biological opinion was issued by the U.S. Fish and Wildlife Service that legally required implementation of a number of reasonable and prudent alternatives to provide conditions for successful natural white sturgeon reproduc-tion in both the braided and meander reaches (U.S. Fish and Wildlife Service, 2006). The channel evaluated for this report was proposed in part to address a requirement in the biologi-cal opinion to implement "permanent structural aquatic habitat features in the Braided Reach by April 1, 2010."

Proposed Channel Design

The channel design used in this analysis is one of several options proposed to improve channel and ecosystem function on the Kootenai River. The design was revised multiple times as project area, boundary conditions, and discharge estimates were refined, and the designers incorporated new ideas. The design presented in this report is not the final design, and its use is intended to be an illustration of the evaluation process rather than an analysis of a final design.

On the basis of meetings with a project group composed of multiple agencies and stakeholders, the channel designer created a list of channel design objectives, which fall into the following categories: (1) create a stable, self-maintaining channel; (2) transport the available sediment; (3) reduce bank erosion and sources of fine sediment; (4) increase stream depth and velocity in the braided reach on the basis of guidance in the biological opinion for the Kootenai River white sturgeon; (5) improve connection to flood plain; (6) reduce flood levels; and (7) protect bridge infrastructure. Although the overall goal of the design was to improve ecosystem integrity in the aquatic and riparian corridor rather than to target the design to

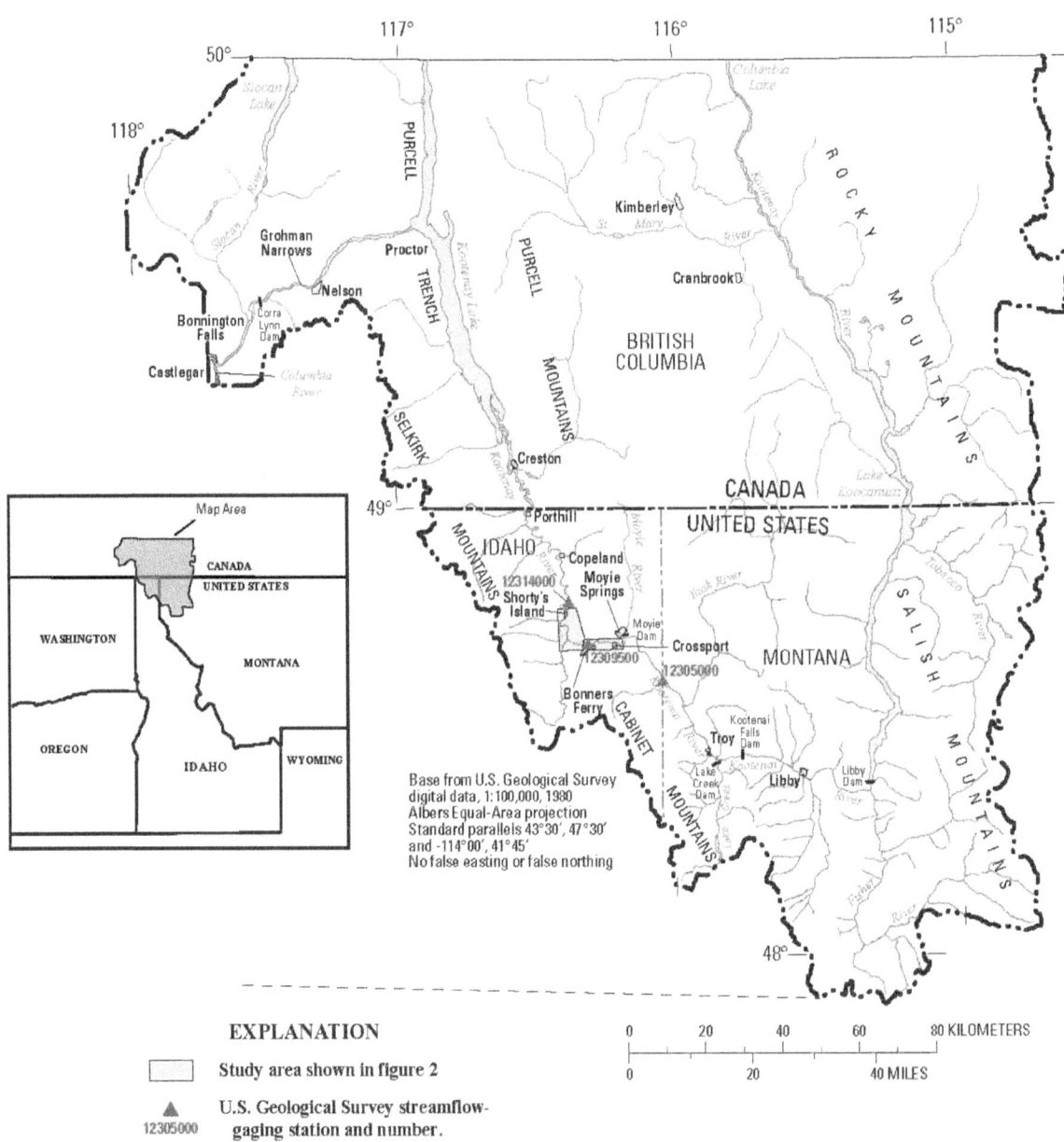

Figure 1. Location of study area near Bonners Ferry, Idaho, and selected streamgaging stations and dams in the Kootenai River drainage basin, Idaho, Montana, and British Columbia, Canada.

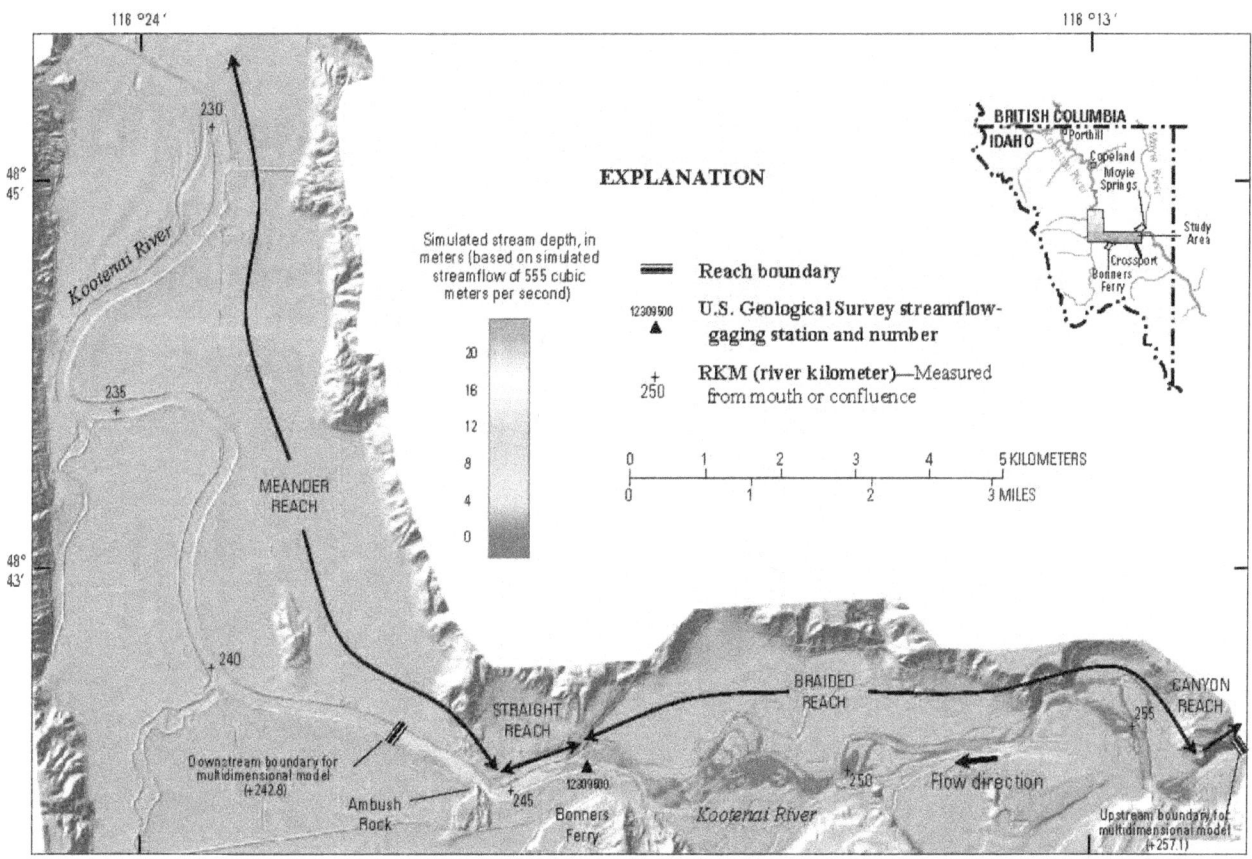

Figure 2. Location of upstream and downstream boundaries for multidimensional flow models, streamgaging station 12309500 Kootenai River at Bonners Ferry, and simulated depth, Kootenai River near Bonners Ferry, Idaho.

one particular species, the endangered status of the Kootenai River white sturgeon required certain features designed specifically to improve spawning aquatic habitat for the sturgeon.

The designer sought to achieve these goals by adjusting the channel geometry to create a channel capable of transporting the available sediment and having the required stream depth and velocity for sturgeon spawning. This resulted in a 34.0-km design channel that started near the upstream end of the braided reach at RKM 256.5 and continued down to RKM 222.5. The most substantial proposed changes occurred in the braided reach of the Kootenai River. The design in that reach converted the quasi-braided channel into a meandering, single-thread, multistage channel. Multistage or compound channels are designed to maintain a low-flow channel that conveys water at all times and adjacent higher flood-plain areas that convey water at higher flows (Tompkins and Kondolf, 2007). Modeling efforts for this report are focused on the braided and straight reach sections of the design channel because of the considerable proposed changes and concerns about sediment transport in those areas. The modeled portion of the design starts in an unaltered portion of the (near the upstream end of

the) braided reach at RKM 257.1 and ends in the upper portion of the meander reach at RKM 242.8 (figs. 1, 2, and 3). The proposed channel in this reach consists of four different elevational surfaces along the river corridor (fig. 4). These surfaces allow the water to spill out onto flood-plain-like features as discharge increases. The lowest surface is the bed of the innermost channel. The next higher surface was designed to match the bankfull discharge of approximately 849.6 m³/s when Kootenay Lake is at lower levels; this surface is therefore termed the "low bankfull surface." The third highest surface is the flood plain at high lake level for bankfull discharges and is termed the "high bankfull surface." The fourth and highest surface is the predam flood plain of the Kootenai River. The design included jettylike structures and v-weirs that were intended to protect the outer banks and concentrate flow in the center portion of the channel to maintain high depths and velocities, which are thought to provide good spawning conditions for sturgeon. In general the design channel is substantially narrower and deeper than the existing Kootenai River channel, and all smaller secondary channels or braids are filled in to form flood-plain features.

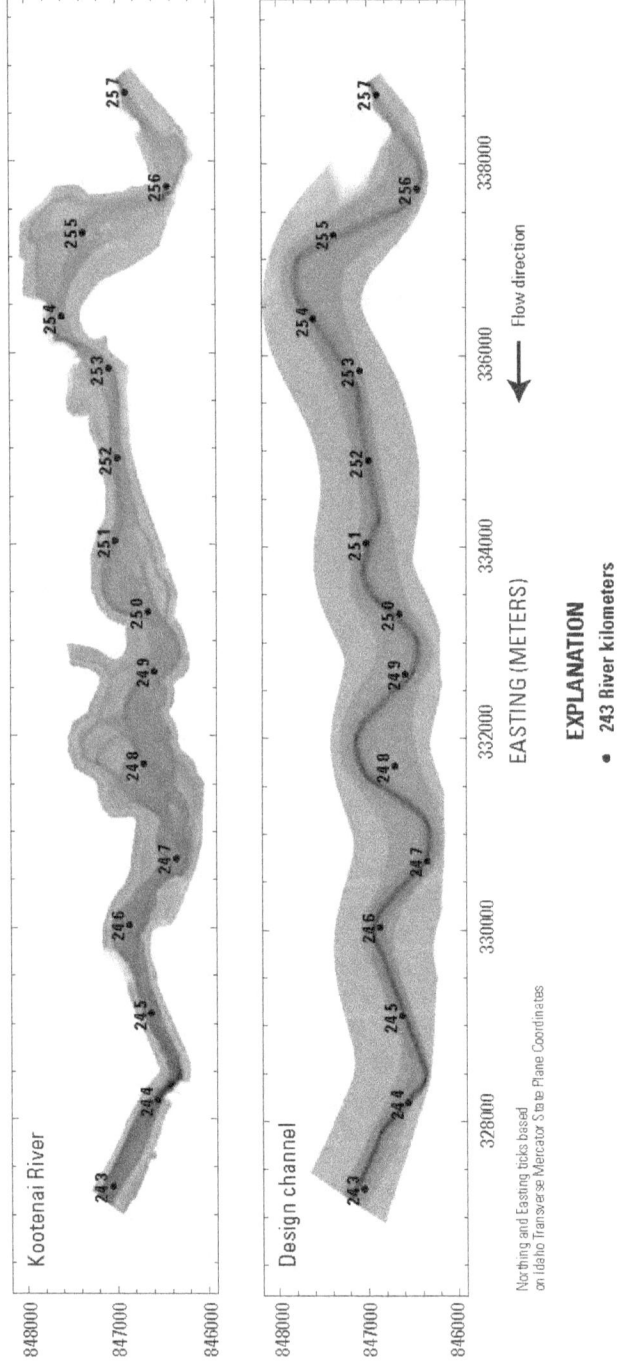

Figure 3. Topography of the Kootenai River and the design channel.

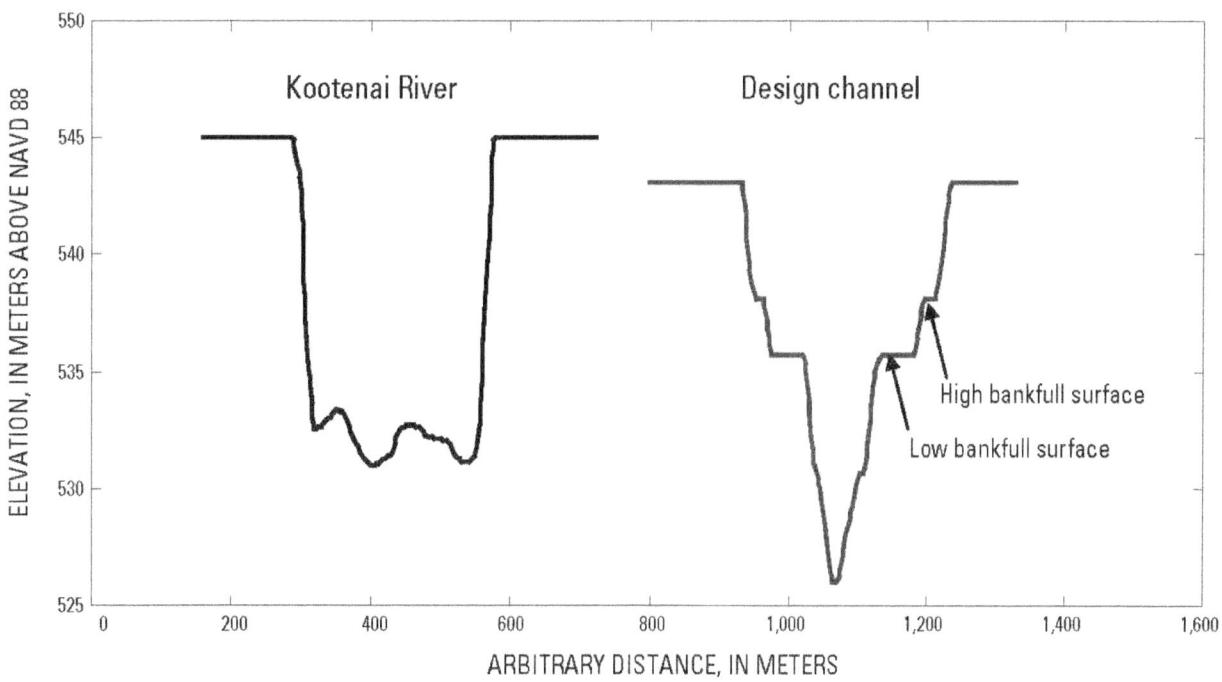

Figure 4.   Example cross sections in the straight reach for the Kootenai River and the design channel. Note multiple bankfull surfaces in the design channel.

Modeling Strategy

Streamflow in the Kootenai River channel and the proposed design channel was simulated in the model to understand how the river channel functions and to discover how altering the channel may change the system for a range of streamflow conditions. The Flow and Sediment Transport with Morphologic Evolution of Channels (FaSTMECH) model (Nelson and McDonald, 1996; see Nelson and others, 2003, for basic equations and numerical methods) in the Multidimensional Surface-Water Modeling System (MD_SWMS) (McDonald and others, 2001; McDonald and others, 2006) was used for this analysis. FaSTMECH is a quasi-three-dimensional model that simulates water-surface elevations, water velocity, boundary shear stress, sediment transport, and bed evolution. Model assumptions are that flow is quasi-steady, incompressible, and hydrostatic, and that turbulence is sufficiently treated by using a simple eddy viscosity Reynolds-stress closure. Minimum model data requirements include detailed channel topography, discharge as a function of time at the upstream boundary, and a water-surface elevation at the downstream boundary for each modeled discharge.

Both the Kootenai River and the design channel were modeled from RKM 257.1 to RKM 242.8 (figs. 2 and 3) starting near what is currently the beginning of the braided reach, through a transition zone called the straight reach, and ending a few kilometers into the meander reach (fig. 2). The

Kootenai River was modeled by using topography measured with real-time global positioning system (GPS) instruments, single-beam and multibeam echo sounders, and light detection and ranging (LIDAR) instruments during several previous and ongoing studies (Barton and others, 2004; Barton and others, 2005). A computational curvilinear grid with 172,200 grid cells approximately 10 m by 10 m was fit to the river channel. The design channel topography was provided in the same coordinate system and supplemented, by the designer, with topography at the upstream end of the reach intended to transition between the existing river channel and the design channel. Streamflow in the design channel was modeled over the same streamwise extent as the Kootenai River channel but with a slightly narrower grid having 135,300 grid cells approximately 10 m by 10 m.

The FaSTMECH model uses lateral eddy viscosity to represent lateral momentum exchange due to turbulence (Nelson and others, 2003). This parameter effectively governs the horizontal diffusivity in the streamflow, which primarily affects the smoothness of the planform velocity structure, especially near banks. The lateral eddy viscosity was calculated by multiplying the average depth by the average width by 0.01 and adjusting the value iteratively. The values determined were consistent with other reported empirical relations (Fischer and others, 1979). Simulations were done until all models converged (meaning that mass and momentum were conserved to a high degree of accuracy at each grid point), which typically occurred after 800 to 2,200 iterations. The following sections discuss the various streamflow conditions and model parameters necessary for this work.

Streamflows and Boundary Conditions

Four discharges—555, 830, 1,311, and 1,841 m³/s—representing moderate flow, design flow, high flow, and floodflow, respectively, were used in both the Kootenai River model and the design channel model simulations. The design discharge was based on the designer's estimate of the bankfull discharge in the study area, which was believed by the project group to be consistent with future managed streamflows below Libby Dam. The design or bankfull discharge was approximately 849.6 m³/s, but a slightly lower discharge of 830 m³/s was evaluated because a water-surface profile along the present reach was available for comparison (Barton and others, 2004; Barton, and others 2005; Berenbrock, 2005; Berenbrock and Bennett, 2005; Berenbrock, 2006; McDonald and others, 2010).

Because the Kootenai River is subject to backwater conditions, each discharge was modeled by using two different downstream boundary conditions to reflect changes in stage caused by relatively high and low Kootenay Lake levels. The modeled stages were interpolated from the 15th and 85th percentile stage for each evaluation discharge by using data from U.S. Geological Survey streamgaging stations Kootenai River at Bonners Ferry (12309500) and Kootenai River at Klockmann Ranch, near Bonners Ferry (12314000; fig. 1). Discharge data are available from the U.S. Geological Survey National Water Information System (*http://waterdata.usgs. gov/nwis*). The post-1994 period of record was used to obtain water-stage data representative of current Libby Dam management practices. For the highest discharge of 1,841 m³/s, the record was extended back to 1965 in order to have enough flow/stage pairs for computing statistics. Once the high and low lake-level stages were established at the gaging stations, stage at the model boundary between the stations was linearly interpolated to provide boundary conditions for the model simulations.

Hydraulic Roughness

Kootenai River

Measured water-surface profiles were used to calibrate the streamflow model for the Kootenai River. Water-surface profiles for a range of discharges were assembled by using stage and discharge data from the Kootenai River at Bonners Ferry gaging station (12309500) and from a series of Hobo pressure transducers installed throughout the braided reach (G.J. Barton, U.S. Geological Survey, unpub. data, 2008). Roughness, as parameterized by the drag coefficient, was calibrated by using the most current water-surface profile measurements available for discharges of 623, 779, 909, 1,042,

1,192, 1,294, and 1,422 m³/s in 2008 and a high discharge of 1,758 m³/s and low discharge of 552 m³/s, both measured in 2006 (table 1). The model was calibrated by adjusting the drag coefficient in 0.0001 increments; values ranged from 0.0027 to 0.0030, using a constant value applied to the entire reach. The final calibrated value was the drag coefficient that produced the lowest root-mean square (RMS) error between the measured and simulated water-surface profile. One water-surface elevation point located 6.4 km from the upstream end of the modeling reach was omitted from the RMS error calculation because it was consistently underpredicted by the model, possibly owing to a datum error in the measurement at that location. At the lowest discharge, the RMS error was 0.037 m. Error increased with increasing discharge to 0.089 m for the second highest discharge modeled. In general, the total water-surface drop and the shape of the water-surface profile (fig. 5) were satisfactorily calibrated by using the constant drag coefficient values listed in table 1. The only exception was the highest discharge of 1,758 m³/s, for which the water-surface profile was overpredicted at the upstream end of the reach and substantially underpredicted at a location 4 km downstream. This disparity could be caused by changing roughness owing to inundation of bars, insufficiently defined topography on high banks near the upstream boundary, or potential errors in the water-surface measurements. Although the disparity is not ideal, these different sources of potential errors could not be resolved without substantial additional effort, and calibration for the highest discharge of 1,758 m³/s was determined to be adequate for this evaluation.

The Kootenai River reach was then modeled using the four selected discharges by using drag coefficients interpolated from the values determined during the initial calibration process (table 2). For the highest modeled discharge of 1,841 m³/s, the closest discharge for which a water-surface profile was available was 1,758 m³/s. The drag coeffiecient calibrated for the 1,758-m³/s discharge was used to model the 1,841 m³/s discharge. The same drag coefficient was used to model both the high and low lake-level conditions for a given discharge. Limited testing showed small changes in the drag coefficient for the same discharge at different lake levels for the existing Kootenai River.

Design Channel

Because the design channel represented a substantial alteration of the river channel over a large spatial area, the roughness of the altered channel was evaluated by calibrating the drag coefficient so that simulated high and low bankfull discharge water surfaces matched the designer's high and low bankfull surfaces. The designer determined these surfaces by using a one-dimensional model that used Manning's *n* values of 0.03 in the main channel and 0.06 in portions of the channel above the low bankfull surface. In this calibration procedure, the same discharge and boundary conditions used by the designer were used, which were different from those specified by the project group for the channel design and evaluation.

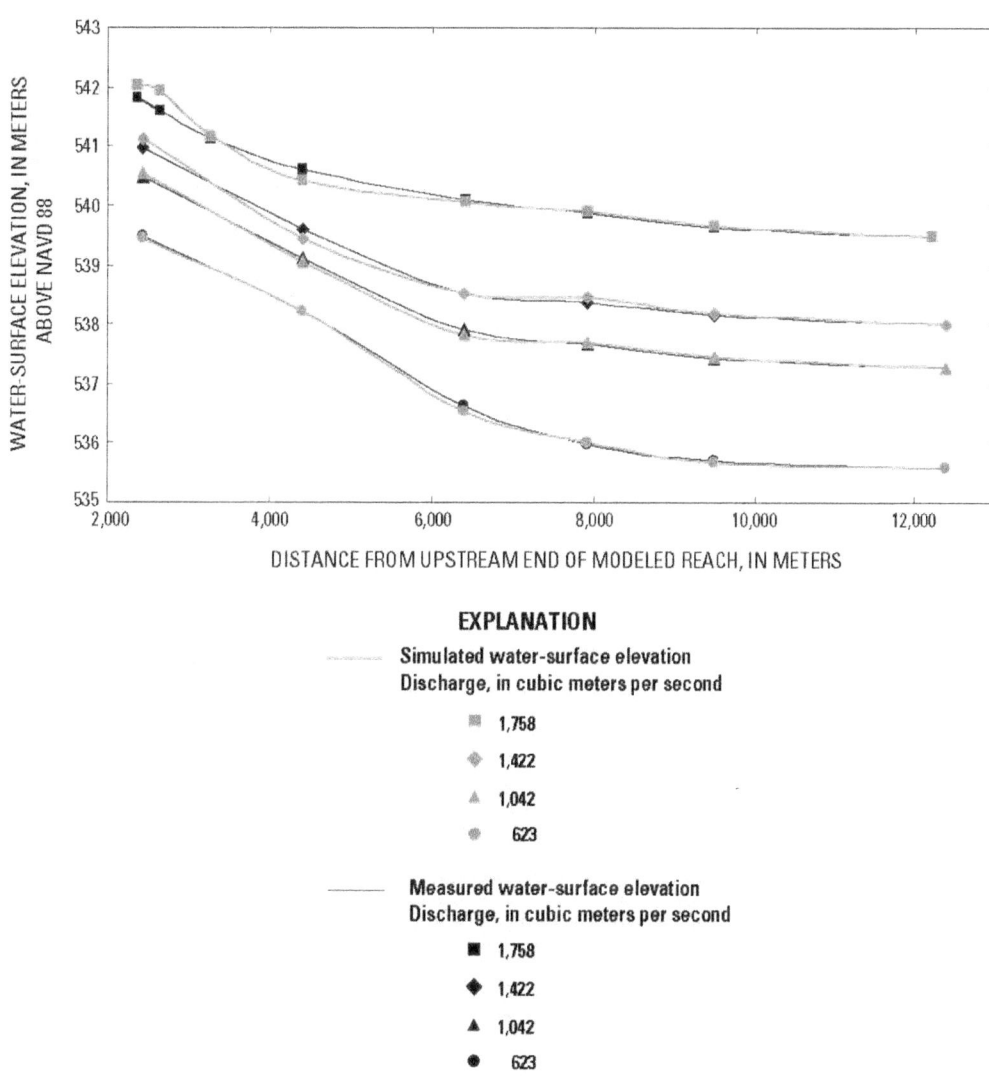

Figure 5. Graph showing example simulated and measured water-surface profiles for selected discharges of the Kootenai River.

The model was calibrated for a discharge of 849.6 m³/s by using boundary conditions that were substantially higher and lower than the water levels selected to approximate the anticipated normal range of Kootenay Lake elevations. The consequences of this design decision are presented in the section "Water-Surface Levels."

Using this method, initial attempts were tried to match the total drop in the water-surface profiles for both bankfull surfaces. However, Froude numbers approaching 1 at the transition between the existing Kootenai River channel and the design channel at the upstream end of the modeled reach caused the simulated water surface in that area to be insensitive to roughness. Therefore, the total water-level drop was matched by using bankfull-surface points in the second bend

near RKM 254.4 (table 3). The drop was matched; however, it was not possible to match the shape of the water-surface profile perfectly to either bankfull water surface. The modeled low-bankfull profile was particularly difficult to match (fig. 6). It could not be determined why the water-surface profiles were shaped so differently without access to the original one-dimensional model used by the designers, so matching the total drop was the best option. The final drag coefficients selected for use in further analysis were 0.0049 for low lake level and 0.0034 for high lake level. These values are larger than the drag coefficients used to model the existing Kootenai River, most likely because the design topography was defined by simple break lines and was extremely smooth compared to the very detailed topography measured in the actual Kootenai

Table 1.   Summary of calibration parameters for the Kootenai River.

[Drag coefficients are based on calibrated values. Lateral eddy viscosity was calculated and adjusted iteratively by using 0.01 × average depth × average velocity; m³/s, cubic meters per second; m, meters; m²/s, square meters per second; RMS, root-mean square]

Measurement date	Discharge (m³/s)	Downstream boundary elevation (m)	Drag coefficient (dimensionless)	Lateral eddy viscosity (m²/s)	Water-surface elevation RMS error (m)
07/05/2006	552	535.62	0.003	0.024	0.037
07/08/2008	623	535.58	0.0024	0.027	0.036
05/15/2008	779	535.48	0.0024	0.031	0.031
06/23/2008	909	536.85	0.0031	0.032	0.060
06/09/2008	1,042	537.28	0.0034	0.035	0.054
06/03/2008	1,192	537.82	0.0035	0.037	0.063
05/20/2008	1,294	537.75	0.0025	0.041	0.091
05/19/2008	1,422	537.99	0.0025	0.043	0.089
06/18/2006	1,758	539.46	0.0028	0.040	[1]0.156

[1]The RMS error drops to 0.078 if two upstreammost points are omitted from the calculation.

Table 2.   Parameters used to model the design channel and the Kootenai River at the evaluation discharges for high and low Kootenay Lake levels.

[m³/s, cubic meters per second; m, meters; m²/s, square meters per second]

Discharge (m³/s)	Kootenay Lake level	Downstream boundary elevation (m)	Design channel		Kootenai River	
			Drag coefficient (dimensionless)	Lateral eddy viscosity (m²/s)	Drag coefficient (dimensionless)	Lateral eddy viscosity (m²/s)
555	High	535.162	0.0034	0.047	0.003	0.024
555	Low	534.556	0.0049	0.047	0.003	0.025
830	High	536.423	0.0034	0.031	0.0027	0.031
830	Low	535.861	0.0049	0.027	0.0027	0.031
1,311	High	538.383	0.0034	0.023	0.0025	0.042
1,311	Low	537.393	0.0049	0.024	0.0025	0.042
1,841	High	540.108	0.0034	0.038	0.0028	0.042
1,841	Low	539.598	0.0049	0.037	0.0028	0.039

Table 3.   Parameters used for the design channel model calibrated to enable matching of simulated bankfull surfaces with design bankfull surfaces on the basis of boundary conditions used by the designer.

[m³/s, cubic meters per second; m, meters; m²/s, square meters per second; RMS, root-mean square]

Discharge (m³/s)	Lake level	Downstream boundary elevation (m)	Initial upstream boundary elevation (m)	Drag coefficient (dimensionless)	Lateral eddy viscosity (m²/s)	RMS error for all points (m)	RMS error of calibration points (m)
846.6	Very high	538.05	545	0.0034	0.024	0.066	0.038
846.6	Very low	535.32	545	0.0049	0.033	0.241	0.017

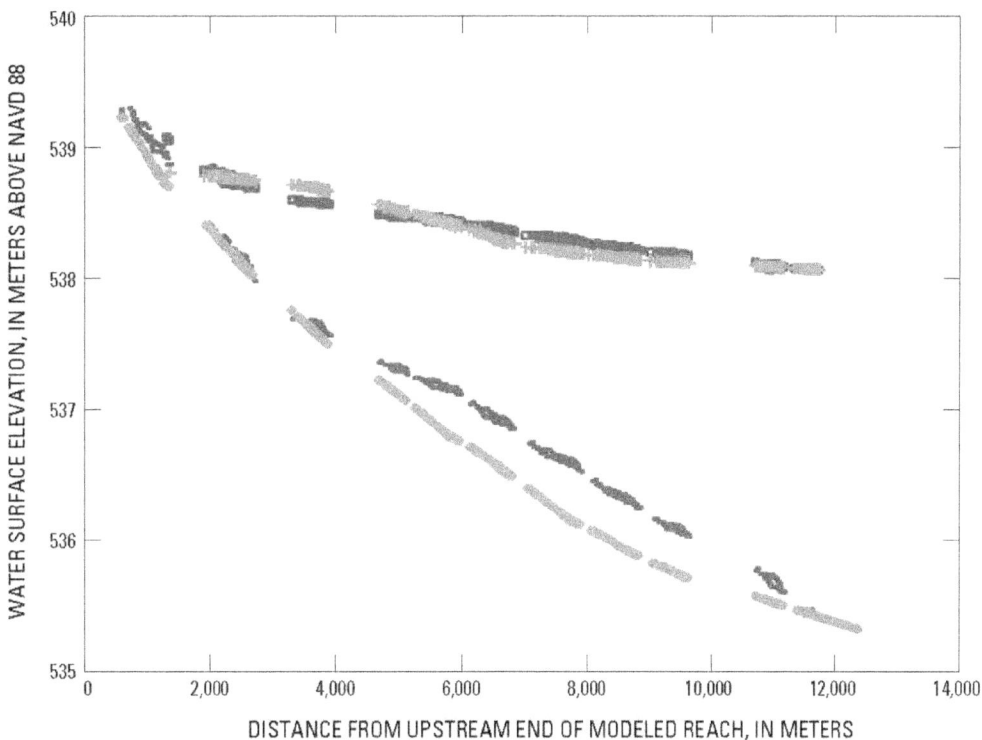

EXPLANATION

- Simulated water-surface elevations—Low lake level; drag coefficient = 0.0049
- Simulated water-surface elevations—High lake level; drag coefficient = 0.0034
- Design high bankfull surface
- Design low bankfull surface

Figure 6.   Graph showing simulated water-surface profiles and design high and low bankfull surfaces for the design channel based on high and low Kootenay Lake levels, a discharge of 849.6 cubic meters per second, and downstream boundary conditions used by designer.

River. Therefore, larger roughness values are required to match simulated water-surface profiles with measured water-surface profiles in the design channel because little or no bed and bank roughness was explicitly defined in the design topography compared to the topography measured for the existing Kootenai River. The high lake-level drag coefficient was used to model all four evaluation discharges during high lake level, and the low lake-level drag coefficient was used to model all four evaluation discharges during low lake level (table 2).

Channel Design Evaluation

The following section presents the method of design-channel evaluation using the preliminary design channel for the Kootenai River. The design channel was evaluated in terms of channel function by focusing on potential (1) water-surface levels, (2) sediment transport, and (3) aquatic habitat characteristics. Only the discharge and lake-level scenarios of most interest are presented for each aspect of channel function.

Results from the Kootenai River modeling are provided where appropriate to explain how the existing system functions and for comparison to the results from the design channel modeling. Results for all discharges and boundary conditions modeled are provided in Appendix 1 in the form of maps of stream depth, velocity, shear stress, Rouse number, and aquatic habitat for two aquatic habitat suitability criteria (HSC) evaluated.

Water-Surface Levels

Simulated water-surface levels for the design channel were compared to the channel morphology. This is necessary to ensure that water surfaces at bankfull discharge will reach the appropriate design bankfull surfaces and to assess whether the channel can convey the floodflow simulated at the high Kootenay Lake level. Simulation results from the bankfull discharge of 830 m³/s at both high and low lake level, and floodflow of 1,841 m³/s at high lake level are compared to the bankfull high surface, the bankfull low surface, and the highest surface of the design channel, respectively. Sensitivity analysis of the simulated water-surface levels to the drag coefficient used in the model also is provided.

For the design channel, the simulated water-surface levels for the bankfull discharge did not match the corresponding elevational surfaces in the channel. If the design channel worked as expected, the simulated water surface at a discharge of 830 m³/s at high Kootenay Lake level should match the high bankfull surface. The simulated water surface, however, was more than 1 m below the high bankfull surface for most of the modeled reach, so that the high bankfull flood plain would not be in contact with the river (fig. 7) at bankfull discharge. Discharges as high as 1,311 m³/s would be required to inundate most of the high bankfull surface. Similarly, the simulated water surface at a discharge of 830 m³/s at low lake level should match the low bankfull surface. The water-surface

levels at that discharge, however, were as much as 0.5 m above the low bankfull surface for most of the modeled reach, with the exception of levels in the upper 3.5 km of the reach, which matched fairly well. This would mean flooding of the bankfull surface at lower discharges than expected. In fact, water levels at a discharge of 555 m³/s at high lake level would reach the low bankfull surface in the lower half of the modeled reach (fig. 7). Flooding the low bankfull surface at lower than anticipated discharges could result in longer floodplain inundation times and increased inundation depths, which could hinder establishment and maintenance of flood-plain riparian communities.

The simulated water-surface levels at 1,841 m³/s at high lake level indicated that the design channel would be able to easily contain the most extreme discharge and lake-level scenario modeled (fig. 7). Under this scenario, the water-surface

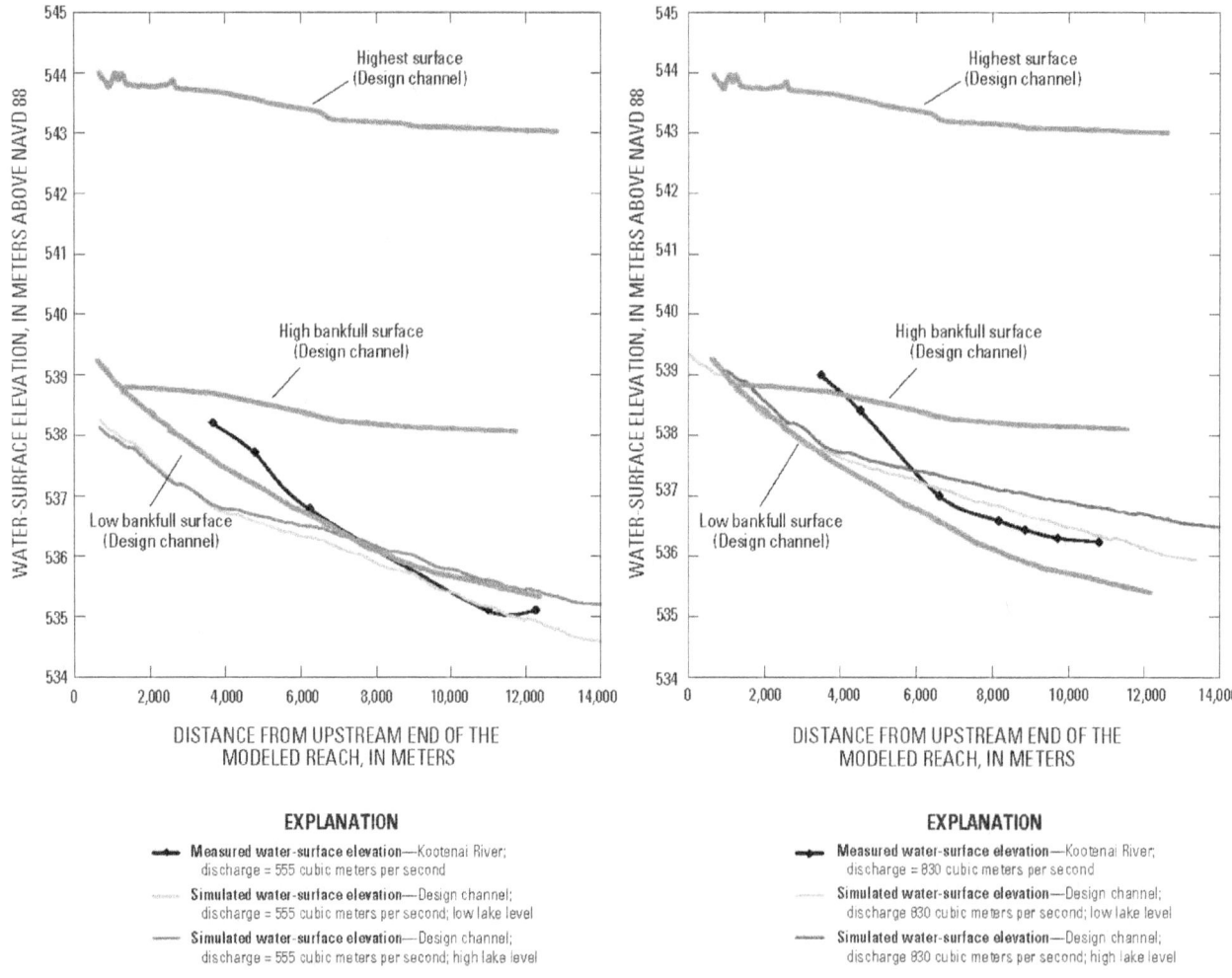

Figure 7.   Graphs showing simulated water-surface profiles for the design channel, based on both high and low Kootenay Lake levels, and measured water surfaces in the Kootenai River, for selected discharges.

level would be more than 2.5 m below the highest surface in the design channel. Thus, even floodflows substantially greater than 1,841 m³/s would not overtop the banks of the design channel. This is in part because the highest surface in the design channel is about 2.5 m higher than the high bankfull surface, which effectively creates a wall or levee to contain substantially higher flows.

The differences between the simulated water surfaces and the design surfaces occurred because different boundary conditions were used to develop the design and to evaluate the design. The high and low boundary conditions based on the 15th and 85th percentile levels of Kootenay Lake were defined to best reflect future lake conditions and were selected by the project group. The designer, however, elected to use more extreme high and low lake boundary conditions in an effort to ensure that no flooding would occur at higher flows. By using

higher lake-level boundary conditions, the designer effectively increased the capacity of the channel beyond the design specifications. Using an exceedingly low lake-level boundary condition in the design, however, resulted in an undersized inner channel that cannot contain flow at the low lake bankfull discharge. The mismatch between the design flood-plain surfaces and the simulated water elevations requires the design to be substantially reworked using more appropriate lake-level boundary conditions.

For illustrative purposes, additional evaluation methods using the Kootenai River restoration design are presented that can be considered for other channel designs. A sensitivity analysis of the simulated water-surface profile was performed by using a range of potential drag coefficients. The coefficients were 200 percent (0.0098) and 50 percent (0.00245) of the calibrated value (0.0049) for a discharge of 830 m³/s at low

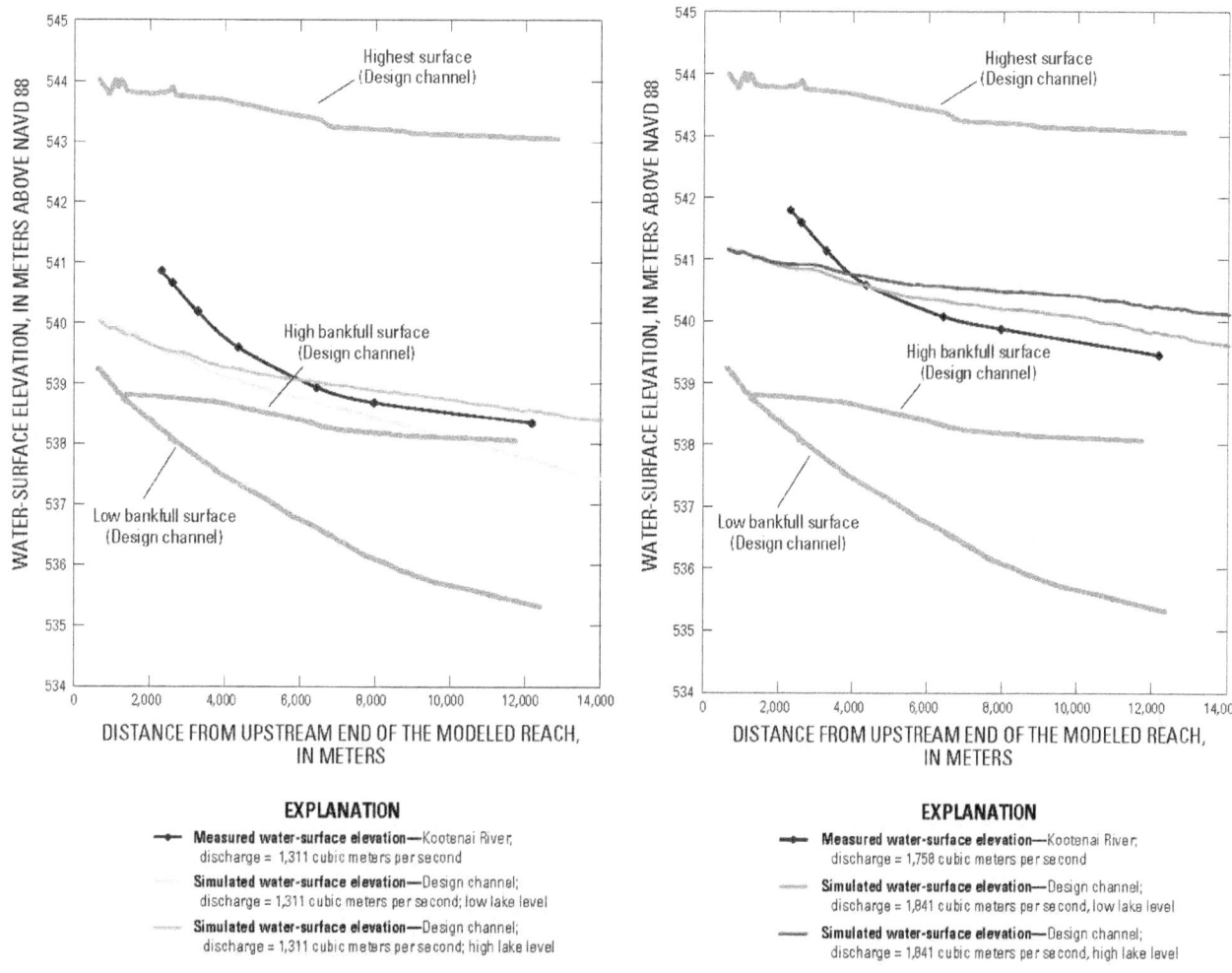

Figure 7. Graphs showing simulated water-surface profiles for the design channel, based on both high and low Kootenay Lake levels, and measured water surfaces in the Kootenai River, for selected discharges.—Continued

lake level. Use of the largest drag coefficient substantially increased water-surface elevations, causing the water surface near the center of the modeled reach to be nearly 1 m above the low bankfull surface (fig. 8). However, the water surface for this large drag coefficient did not overtop the high bankfull surface or match the measured Kootenai River water-surface profile. Use of the smallest drag coefficient lowered the water-surface profile, but the water surface remained above the designed low bankfull surface except at the upstreammost points. The channel would also be capable of conveying the highest discharge modeled, 1,841 m³/s, without flooding if the drag coefficient were 200 percent of the calibrated value.

The drag coefficient necessary for a match of the upstreammost water-surface elevations measured was determined in order to see how much rougher the channel would need to be for water levels to match those in the existing Kootenai River. A drag coefficient of 0.027 (about 5.5 times larger than the calibrated value) was required to match the existing water-surface drop. Because it is unlikely that the constructed channel will have a roughness this much greater than either the roughness used to model the design channel or the roughness of the existing Kootenai River, the water-surface profile in the upper portion of the braided reach would be substantially lower than it is in the existing Kootenai River channel.

Sediment Transport

Sediment transport for the existing Kootenai River and the design channel were evaluated in terms of sediment mobility and sediment transport mode, which provide information about channel stability. The mobility of gravel-sized material was based on the D_{50} sediment in the braided reach. Transport of gravel in the braided reach is an important driver for the current channel morphology and will be critical for

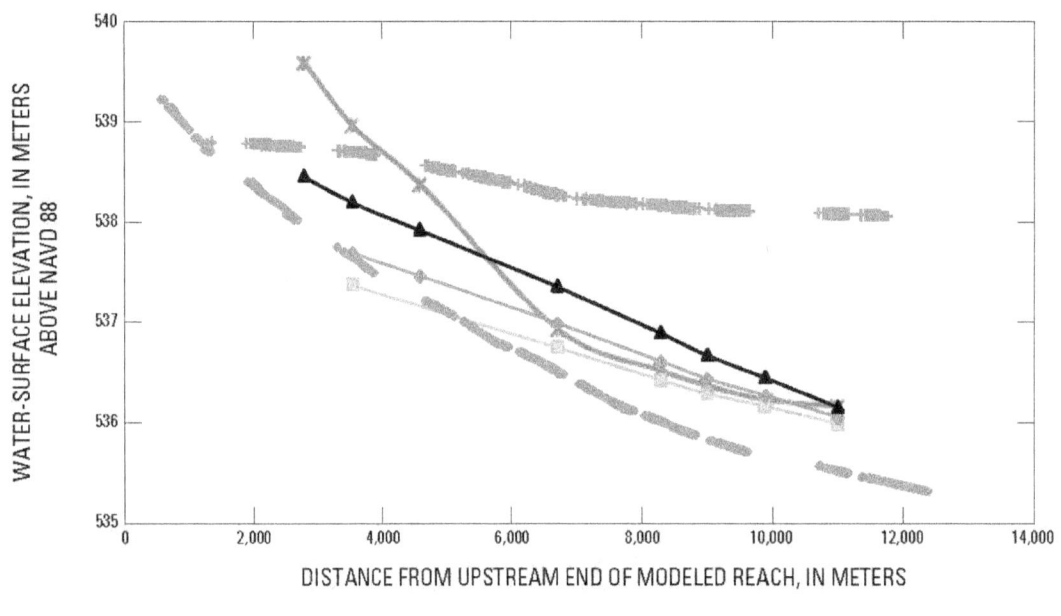

EXPLANATION

— Measured water-surface elevation—Kootenai River, 2006;
    discharge = 830 cubic meters per second

— Simulated water-surface elevation—Design channel;
    discharge = 830 cubic meters per second; roughness coefficient = 0.00245

— Simulated water-surface elevation—Design channel;
    discharge = 830 cubic meters per second; roughness coefficient = 0.0049

— Simulated water-surface elevation—Design channel;
    discharge = 830 cubic meters per second; roughness coefficient = 0.0098

+   High bankfull surface—Design channel

    Low bankfull surface—Design channel

Figure 8.   Graph showing sensitivity of the simulated water-surface profile for the design channel, based on a discharge of 830 cubic meters per second at low Kootenay Lake level to three different roughness coefficients, with water-surface profile for the Kootenai River measured in 2006 included for comparison.

maintaining channel geometry in the design channel. The transport mode of finer sand-sized material was evaluated based on the D_{50} sediment in the meander reach. The transport mode of sand in the meander reach indicates whether or not sand dunes will be present on the bed, a condition that is potentially detrimental to spawning sturgeon.

In the sediment mobility section, analysis is focused on the bankfull discharge of 830 m³/s and the flood discharge of 1,841 m³/s. Transport mode is discussed in general terms for all discharges modeled because there were only subtle changes in transport mode with changes in discharge. For both sections, simulation results based on low lake-level boundary conditions are the focus because higher lake levels cause more extensive backwater conditions in the braided reach, inhibiting sediment transport. The sensitivity of simulated sediment mobility and transport mode to different drag coefficients for the design channel is presented.

Sediment Mobility

Sediment mobility was evaluated by determining the critical shear stress required for initial motion of the coarse sediment currently found in the braided reach of the Kootenai River. Gravel transport was evaluated using the D_{50} sediment determined as the arithmetic mean of the D_{50} from nine Wolman pebble counts measured throughout the braided reach (R.L. Fosness, U.S. Geological Survey, unpub. data, 2008). The D_{50} of the braided reach is 3.4-cm gravel, which has a calculated critical shear stress of 0.029 (dimensionless) on the basis of equations in Parker and others (2003). Initial motion was evaluated because shear stress throughout the existing river is low compared to the stress necessary to move gravel. The critical shear stress necessary for initial motion gravel was calculated as

$$\tau^* = \frac{\tau_{cr}}{(\rho_s - \rho) g D_{50}} \qquad (2)$$

where τ_{cr} is the dimensionless critical shear stress determined by using equations in Parker and others (2003), ρ_s is the density of the sediment, ρ is the density of water, and g is the acceleration of gravity. The calculated value of τ_{cr} used in this report and three other commonly reported τ_{cr} values and related τ_* for each are provided in table 4. The analysis focuses on the bankfull and flood-level discharges at low lake level.

Simulated shear stress for the Kootenai River was highest near the upstream end of the modeled reach and decreased with distance downstream for the discharges of 830 m³/s and 1,841 m³/s (fig. 9). At the bankfull discharge (830 m³/s), gravel was mobile only in small patches (shear stress greater than 15.5 N/m²). One small patch of mobility (about 30 by 26 m) was located near RKM 255.6, and another small patch (50 by 15 m) was located near RKM 254. Three larger patches were located between RKM 249.5 and RKM 250.5; these are all about 140 by 50 m. The small values of shear stress simulated throughout the present Kootenai River suggests negligible

Table 4. Four different dimensionless critical shear stress values and the resulting critical shear stress values for D_{50} sediment (3.4 centimeters) in the braided reach of the Kootenai River.

[D_{50}, mean sediment grain size diameter; N/m², newtons per square meter]

Critical dimensionless shear stress, τ_{cr}	Critical shear stress, τ^*, for D_{50} sediment (N/m²)
0.029*	15.5*
0.03	16.1
0.045	24.2
0.06	32.3

*values used to evaluate mobility in this report.

transport of gravel-size material at this discharge, even under low Kootenay Lake level.

At the highest modeled discharge of 1,841 m³/s, the Kootenai River can transport gravel down to RKM 251 with a large gap between RKM 254 and RKM 256 (fig. 9). Higher flows, therefore, can transport gravel over a larger area of the channel but were still unable to move this sediment through most of the modeled reach. The change in slope between the canyon reach and the meander reach causes a rapid reduction in shear stress throughout the study area. When the stress becomes insufficient to move the incoming sediment, the material is deposited, which causes the river to be quasi-braided. Larger sediment grains currently found farther downstream in the braided reach were likely transported by substantially larger streamflows that occurred before Libby Dam was built.

In the design channel, shear stress was highest near the upstream end of the reach and decreased downstream. The design reach modeled at the low bankfull discharge of 830 m³/s would be capable of moving gravel from the upstream end of the reach down to about RKM 253.5. Between the upstream end of the reach and RKM 253.5, there would be a few segments in the bends where the stress would be too low to move this sediment (fig. 9). Below RKM 253.5, the stress would be higher than the stress in the Kootenai River at the same discharge but still insufficient to move gravel-size sediment.

At the highest modeled discharge of 1,841 m³/s at low lake level, overall shear stress in the design channel would be lower than at bankfull discharge. This is because the modeled design causes backwater conditions to form in the vicinity of the sinusoidal meander bends near RKM 248. The reduced shear stress would move gravel only from the upstream end of the reach down to about RKM 256. The intermediate discharge of 1,311 m³/s does not appear to cause backwater conditions, and shear stress for this discharge would be higher than that for the bankfull discharge.

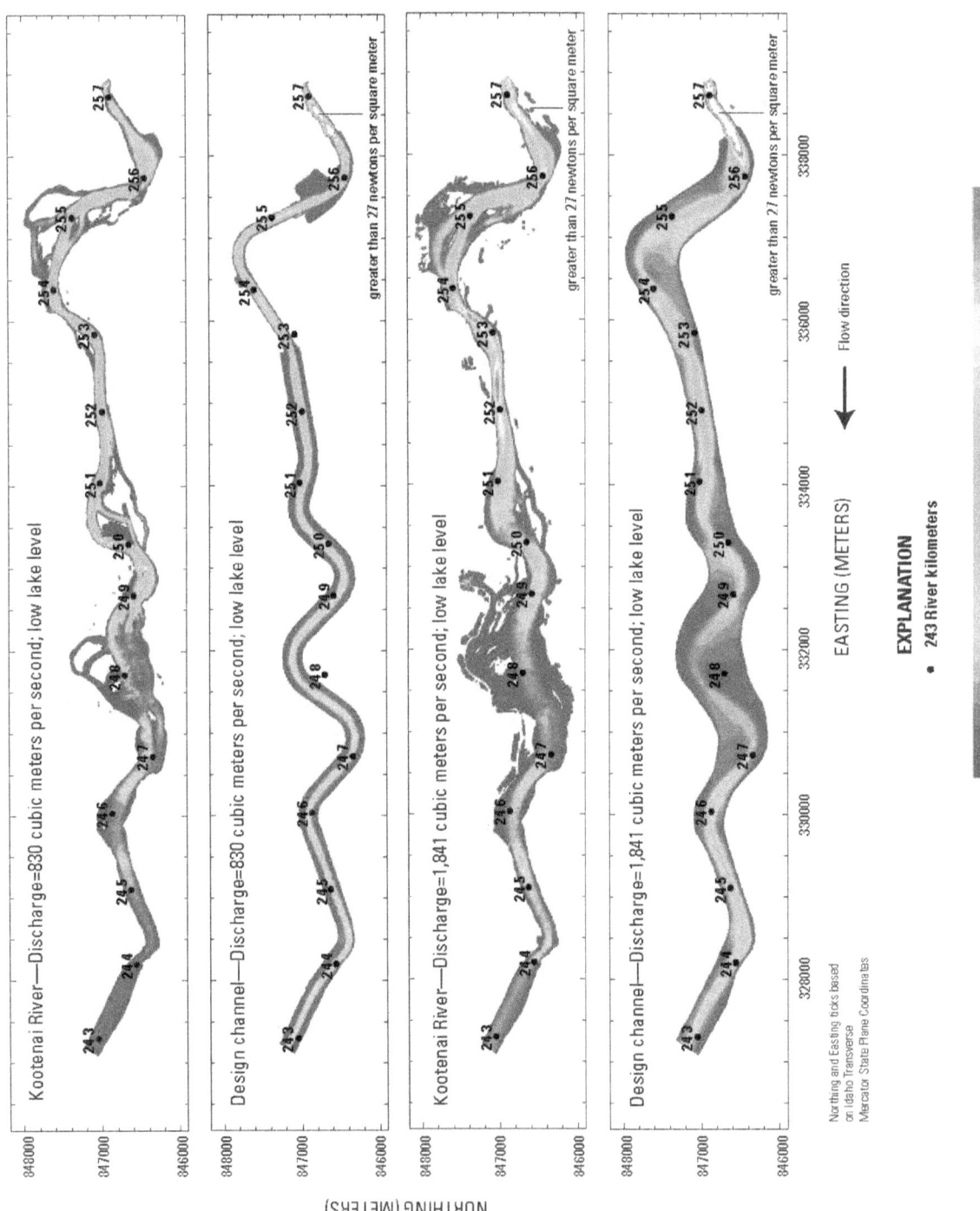

Figure 9.   Simulated shear stress for the Kootenai River and the design channel for discharges of 830 and 1,841 cubic meters per second at low Kootenay Lake level.

Both the design channel and the Kootenai River had the highest shear stresses near the upstream end of the modeled reach, and stresses decreased downstream. The longitudinal gradient in shear stress would reduce transport of the gravel in the downstream direction. In the Kootenai River, this results in deposition of bed material leading to the existing quasi-braided conditions. The design channel may be better able to move smaller gravels farther downstream owing to somewhat higher shear stresses in downstream areas of the channel relative to the Kootenai River. However, any gravel-size material delivered to the design reach will likely be deposited in the reach, and the design may only shift the location of this depositional zone farther downstream. Deposition of material in the design reach has the potential to change the constructed river channel through time. Field studies of bedload transport in the existing Kootenai River are underway to quantify the volume and size of sediment delivered to the braided reach (Fosness and Williams, 2009). These data could be used to understand the rate of potential deposition in the design channel or to redesign the channel to accommodate the sediment load.

Sensitivity analysis in this study showed that simulated sediment transport in the design channel was fairly responsive to the drag coefficient used to model the reach. Larger drag coefficients increased the stress on the bed, given that $\tau = \rho C_d (u^2 + v^2)$, where C_d is the drag coefficient, and u and v are horizontal components of velocity. At a discharge of 830 m³/s at low lake level, for example, 200 percent of the calibrated drag coefficient produced stress sufficient to move gravel down to RKM 251 almost continuously and to move it sporadically through the straight reach and into the meander reach (about RKM 246 to RKM 242.2). One-half of the calibrated drag coefficient only produced shear stress adequate to move gravel for the first 700 m of the modeled reach.

Transport Mode

The transport mode of finer sediment like sand controls conditions on the bed of the existing Kootenai River, which may be important for successful spawning by sturgeon. In the lower half of the straight reach and in the meander reach of the Kootenai River, large-scale dune fields form on the bed at discharges in which sand moves as bedload (Barton and others, 2005). As discharge increases, the sand becomes entrained and moves in suspension, which may cause the dunes to wash out. Video surveillance of the bed after exceptionally high streamflows in 2006 showed bare gravel in portions of the meander reach, suggesting that the dunes had washed out and the accumulated fine sediment overlying the lag gravel deposits had eroded (McDonald and others, 2010). Models of the Kootenai River and design channel extend from the braided reach into the meander reach, allowing some inferences to be made about the transport mode of fine sand through these areas.

Rouse numbers were used to indicate the transport mode of sand size sediment currently found in the meander reach of the Kootenai River. The D_{50} of the meander reach (0.023 cm) was used to characterize the sediment as sand for this analysis.

Streamflow in the main channel of the braided reach moved the sand fully in suspension until about RKM 248.5 (Rouse number less than 0.8); then the sand moved in partial suspension until the end of the braided reach between RKM 245 and RKM 246 (Rouse number 0.8–1.2). This was true for all discharges examined (fig. 10). Rouse numbers were higher in the side channels of the braided reach, indicating that the sand would move through those areas as bedload. In the straight reach, the sand moved at some level of suspension for all discharges, and the sand was fully in suspension in a greater portion of the channel as discharge increased. In the meander reach, the sand moved as bedload near the channel margins and at low levels of suspension near the center of the channel at low discharges. As discharge increased, more of the sand in the meander reach moved in suspension, and at 1,841 m³/s, most of the sand was in suspension through the end of the modeled reach. This result substantiates field evidence that dunes wash out in this area at very high discharge.

In the thalweg of the design channel, Rouse numbers indicated sand moved in full suspension at all discharges (fig. 10). The only exception occurred for the discharge of 1,841 m³/s, in which Rouse numbers indicate the sand was in partial suspension for a short section (RKM 247 to 249). Thus, sand dunes would be unlikely to compose the bed of the design channel. As discharge increased and river water inundated the flood plain, sand in suspension would be concentrated very close to the bed or move as bedload in some areas of the flood plain. This, together with low shear stress values, indicates that fine-grained sediment could be deposited on the flood plain.

The transport mode for the design channel does not appear to be sensitive to changes in the drag coefficient. In the design channel, at one-half the calibrated drag coefficient for the 830 m³/s discharge at low lake level, less area would be inundated and sediment would move as bedload along a wider area on the channel margin compared to that for the calibrated drag coefficient. At twice the calibrated drag coefficient, when more area of the channel would be inundated, the sand would be in suspension throughout a greater portion of the main channel.

Aquatic Habitat

Modeling results from both the Kootenai River and the design channel were evaluated for the Kootenai River white sturgeon by using two different sets of aquatic Habitat Suitability Criteria (HSC). The first set of HSC was developed from habitat needs for spawning Kootenai River white sturgeon identified in the U.S. Fish and Wildlife Service biological opinion (U.S. Fish and Wildlife Service, 2006; U.S. Fish and Wildlife Service, 2008). This criterion, termed "BiOp," assigns a suitability of 1 to all areas where the stream depth is greater than or equal to 7.01 m and the velocity is greater than or equal to 1.0 m/s. Areas that do not meet these thresholds are assigned a suitability of 0. The second HSC used, termed "modeled spawning locations" (MSL), was developed through

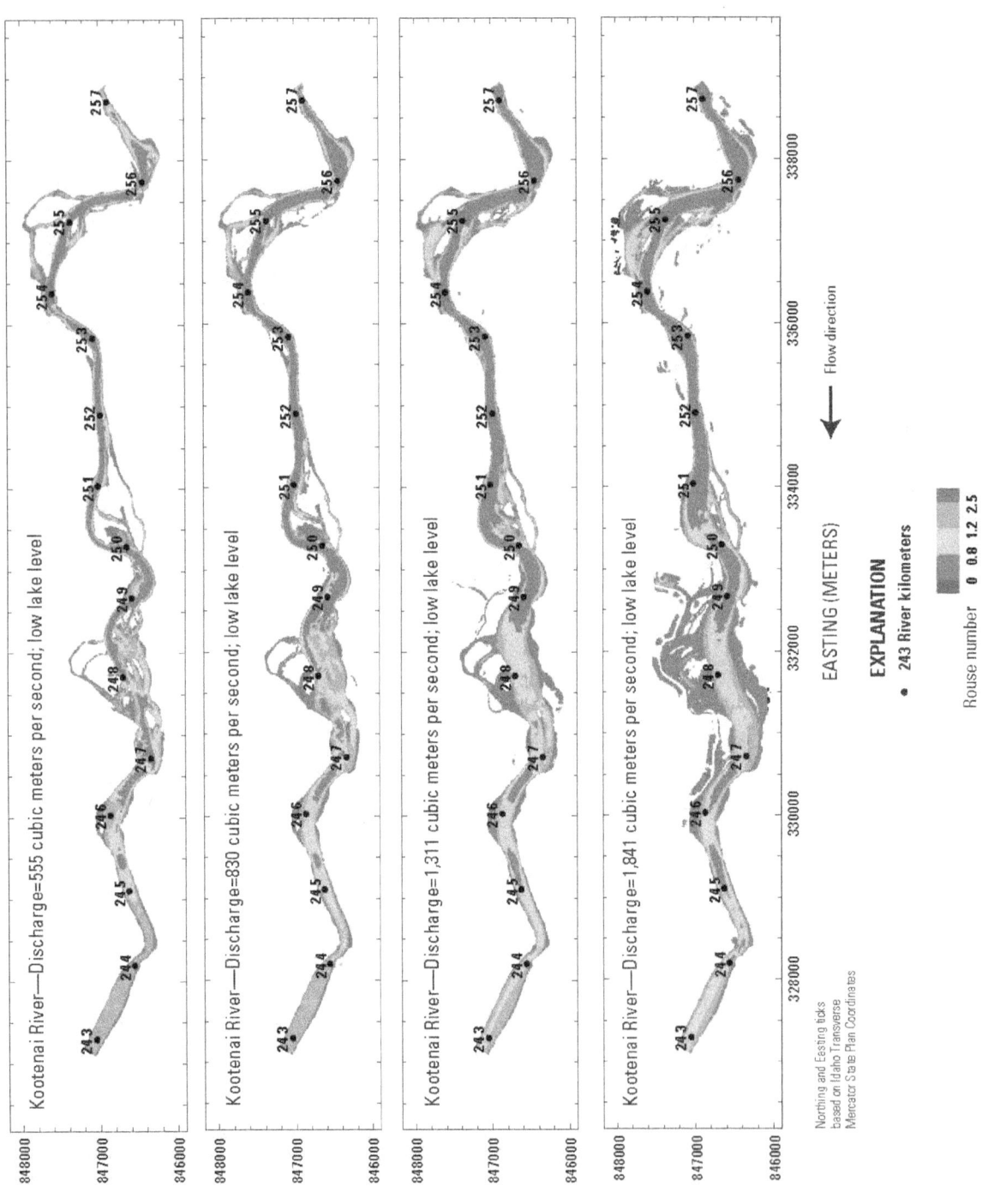

Figure 10. Model-calculated Rouse number for all simulated discharges at low Kootenay Lake levels for the Kootenai River and the design channel.

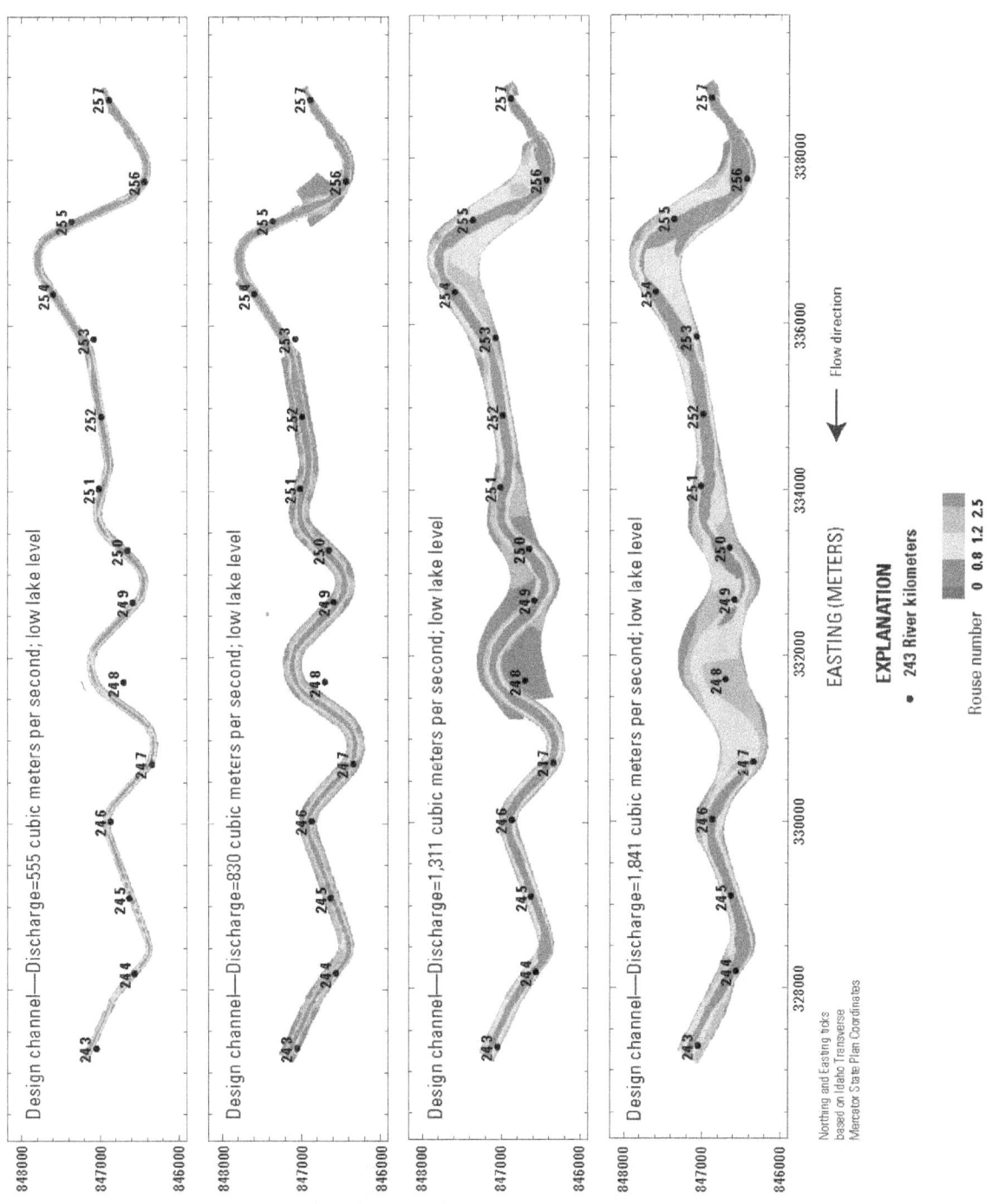

NORTHING (METERS)

EASTING (METERS)

Flow direction

EXPLANATION

• 243 River kilometers

Rouse number   0 0.8 1.2 2.5

Northing and Easting trids
based on Idaho Transverse
Mercator State Plan Coordinates

Figure 10. Model-calculated Rouse number for all simulated discharges at low Kootenay Lake levels for the Kootenai River and the design channel.—Continued

previous work that modeled depth and velocity at locations where sturgeon eggs have been found in the meander reach of the Kootenai River (McDonald and others, 2010). The MSL criterion is therefore a proxy for preferred spawning locations; the criteria curves for depth and velocity are shown in figure 11. Neither HSC evaluates substrate, which is typically an important component in spawning success. Analysis of the weighted usable area (WUA) for all four discharges modeled is presented to show the change in WUA with discharge.

In general, the WUA for the design channel was larger than that for the Kootenai River for both the MSL and the BiOp aquatic habitat criterion (fig. 12). The largest WUA values typically occurred in the design channel at the discharge of 1,311 m³/s. In the design channel, the peak in WUA occurred at that discharge for three of the four HSC curves and decreased at the highest discharged modeled. The WUA for the Kootenai River increased as discharge increased, peaking at the highest discharge modeled, 1,841 m³/s. The WUA for the Kootenai River increased by a factor of 3 between 555 m³/s and 1,841 m³/s for the MSL criterion and increased by a factor of 27 between the same discharges for the BiOp criterion. At the highest discharge modeled, the WUA available in the design channel and the Kootenai River were comparable. The WUA calculated for the MSL criterion was greater than that calculated for the BiOp criterion for both channels, which indicates that the requirements in the BiOp criterion are more narrowly defined than the range of conditions in which the sturgeon currently spawn. Results at high lake level and low lake level were similar, except that the low lake level WUA for the design channel MSL criterion peaked at the discharge of 1,841 m³/s rather than at 1,311 m³/s for the design channel.

The spatial distribution of aquatic habitat for these flows showed differing levels of aquatic habitat connectivity depending on the HSC, stream discharge, and lake level. In general, the aquatic habitat available in the Kootenai River is more patchy and discontinuous than in the design channel (figs. 13 and 14). As discharge increases, the aquatic habitat connectivity increases for both channel configurations. Aquatic habitat suitability based on the BiOp criterion was patchier because the BiOp criterion is a binary function with specific thresholds for depth and velocity; cells were either suitable or unsuitable with no in-between values. The MSL criteria developed from the egg location data produce aquatic habitat suitability that ranges from 0 to 1, which means that marginal aquatic habitat is shown in the maps and included in the WUA calculation.

Another way to look at potential created aquatic habitat for a channel design is to use simple histograms to evaluate depth and velocity distribution. As shown in figure 15, the design channel had a more uniform depth distribution and more deep areas than the existing Kootenai River. The braided reach of the Kootenai River had more area with higher velocity flow, but the river and the design channel contained about the same area of channel with velocities near the target of 1.0 m/s.

Considerations for Channel Design Evaluations

This evaluation of the preliminary channel design for the Kootenai River restoration found several flaws that may be addressed in future design revisions. Analysis of the water-surface levels showed that the low bankfull flood plain would be submerged by as much as 0.5 m at a discharge similar to that of bankfull discharge. However, the high bankfull flood plain would be inaccessible during any likely Kootenay Lake level at bankfull discharge. Sediment transport analysis found that the design channel would be largely unable to move the D₅₀ sediment through the reach at the low bankfull discharge. Therefore, the design channel morphology will likely adjust through time because of deposition of sediment in the reach. In addition, the design channel would be less competent than the existing Kootenai River at moving sediment at extremely high discharges owing to unforeseen backwater conditions developing in the design channel. The transport mode calculations indicate that deposition of fine sand should not occur in the design channel, although deposition on the flood plain would be possible. Despite substantial problems in the physical function of the design channel, the design would create more aquatic habitat suitable for spawning sturgeon at lower discharges (based on the two HSC evaluated) than is currently available in the Kootenai River.

The design channel did not function as anticipated primarily because the boundary conditions used in design development were more extreme than the boundary conditions selected by the project group to reflect the potential range in future Kootenay Lake levels. Therefore, if this type of channel reconfiguration is desired, the design could be improved by using boundary conditions that are consistent with the best estimates of future conditions. Redesigning the channel should eliminate or reduce the mismatch between the simulated water-surface profile and the bankfull surfaces. Flood-plain connectivity would likely be improved, and the depth and duration of flood-plain inundation would better support a riparian plant community. The redesign could potentially result in increased sediment transport through the reach at all discharges. This may better maintain the topography of the design channel but could lead to deposition of gravel downstream in the river. A redesigned channel would also likely increase the quantity and quality of aquatic habitat available (based on the HSC evaluated) for fish at lower discharges in comparison to the aquatic habitat currently available in the Kootenai River.

Multidimensional Modeling Considerations

A number of factors were identified in this evaluation that could be considered when developing or evaluating a channel design. First, extensive data on existing channel conditions makes the design and evaluation process more robust. Second, application of multidimensional modeling and analysis requires very detailed channel designs. Third, there are several

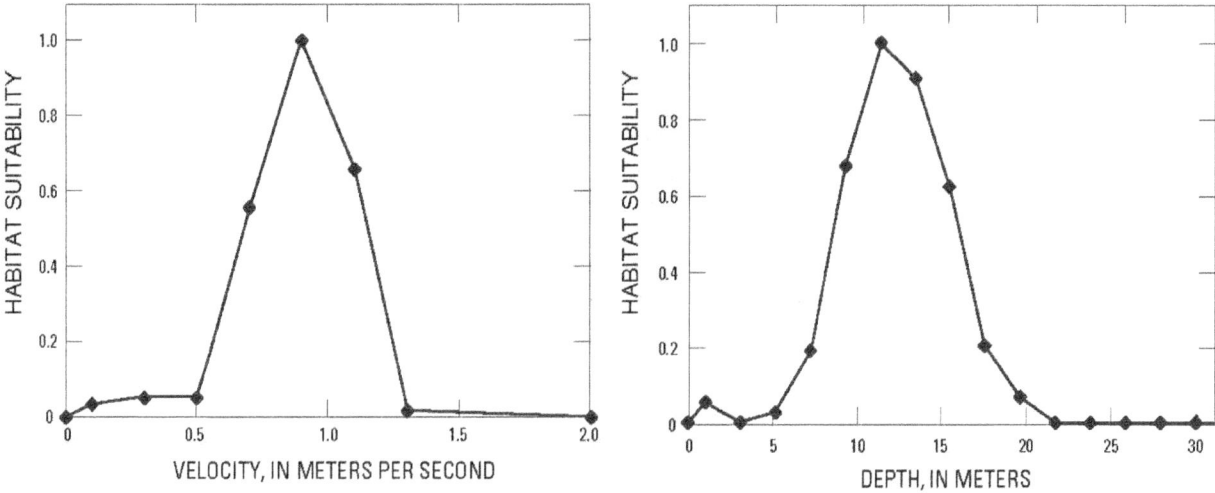

Figure 11.   Graphs showing modeled spawning location (MSL) criteria developed from modeled stream velocity and depths at locations where sturgeon eggs were recovered in the Kootenai River.

important sources of uncertainty when modeling channels that have not been constructed. Finally, multidimensional models can be used for additional analyses to better assess channel function and long-term stability.

Data Requirements for Channel Design and Design Evaluation

Physical information about the existing river system is crucial for effective restoration-channel design and evaluation. For example, detailed topographic maps of the Kootenai River helped guide the channel design and allowed the design channel and the Kootenai River channel to be compared in terms of the project goals. Identification of an appropriate design discharge that will be consistent with future conditions and channel morphology is critical. Other critical information helpful in channel design and evaluation include water-surface profiles for known discharges, sediment-size distributions, and bedload measurements. In addition, the average hydrograph, flood-frequency curves, and sediment loads provide valuable information that can be incorporated into the design to ensure the channel will function throughout a range of conditions and sediment loads. Finally, information about historical channel conditions, land-use changes, and bank-erosion rates, for example, provides insight into the type of channel that will likely achieve the desired goals.

Channel Design Requirements for Multidimensional Modeling

Multidimensional modeling of channel designs requires a sufficient level of design detail. The design needs to include a high-resolution three-dimensional surface of the design channel rather than simple planview drawings and selected example cross sections. The topography should sufficiently define the bed and banks as well as any channel structures such as hooks and weirs. The design also needs to include transitional topography between the design channel and the unaltered portions of the river. In the channel evaluated in this study, an abrupt transition caused a hydraulic jump to form near the upstream end of the modeled reach at RKM 256.7 at a discharge of 555 m³/s (fig. 16). The designer's estimate of the channel roughness also needs to be included in the final design as well as the planned water-surface profile at the design discharge and the boundary conditions used to develop the design if applicable. These data can aid in developing multidimensional models and allow for comparisons between the modeled results and the intended function of the design.

Sources of Uncertainty in Modeling Results and Design-Channel Function

Many sources of uncertainty hinder the ability to explicitly simulate how a design channel will function and whether or not the channel will be stable through time. Some sources of uncertainty relate to potential unforeseen changes in streamflow or sediment conditions. Additional sources are related to the design itself, including uncertainty about the final roughness of the constructed channel and whether or not the proposed construction techniques will be feasible and durable.

Future Streamflow and Sediment Conditions

Future streamflow conditions could determine design success. Where extensive long-term gage records are available,

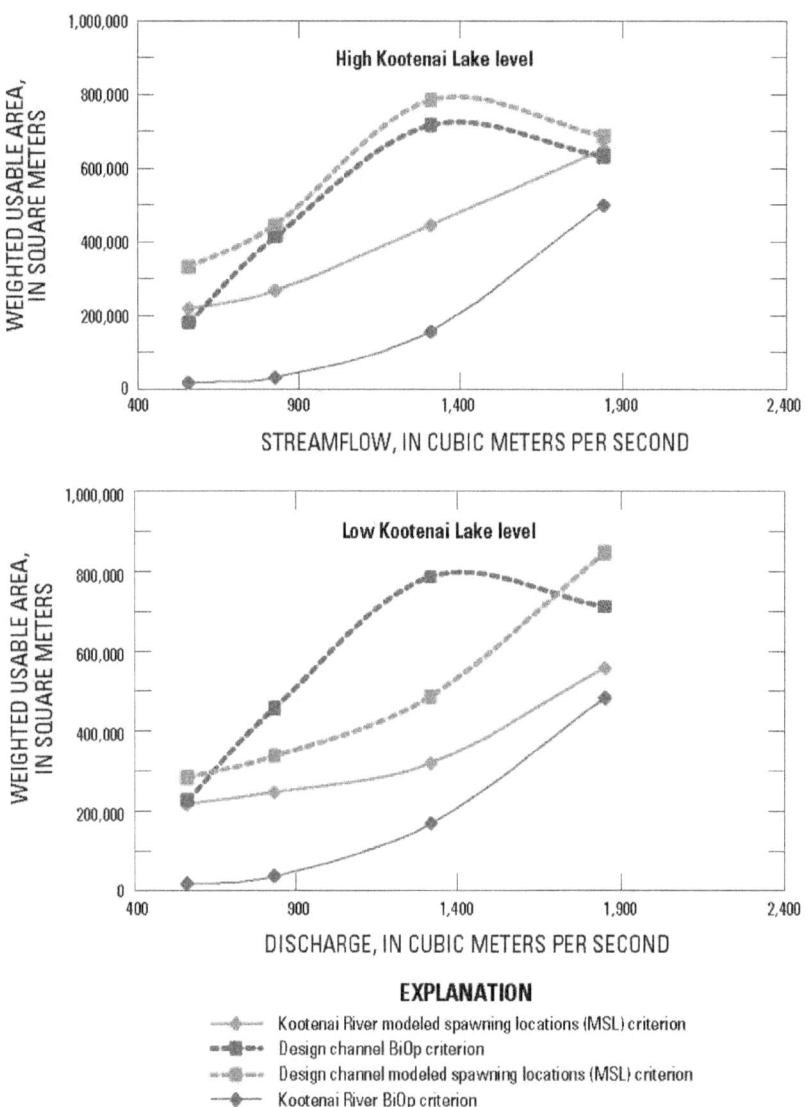

Figure 12.   Graphs showing weighted usable area calculated using simulations of the Kootenai River and the Design channel for the BiOp and the modeled spawning locations (MSL) criterion.

confidence about the range of potential streamflow conditions is high. In many cases where streamflow is unregulated, however, records are either short or nonexistent, which makes determining suitable design discharges difficult and increases uncertainty about the potential range of discharges for that system. Furthermore, in many cases the flow regime has been changed by dams or water-withdrawal systems, which may be operated differently in the future to address different water demands. Finally, climate change may affect future streamflows, resulting in higher or lower streamflow or more extreme flow conditions. Each of these factors has the potential to create either higher or lower than expected flows that could alter

the constructed channel compromising sediment transport, aquatic habitat, and flood-plain connectivity.

Future sediment loads could be different from those anticipated owing to either errors or uncertainties in initial measurements prior to channel construction, or to changes in sediment sources upstream and the streamflows that deliver that sediment. Accurate bedload measurements are relatively difficult to make in the field, particularly at the most important higher discharges, because of safety concerns and spatial and temporal variability in sediment transport. These potential sources of error can increase the uncertainty in bedload measurements and sediment-load rating curves used to develop the

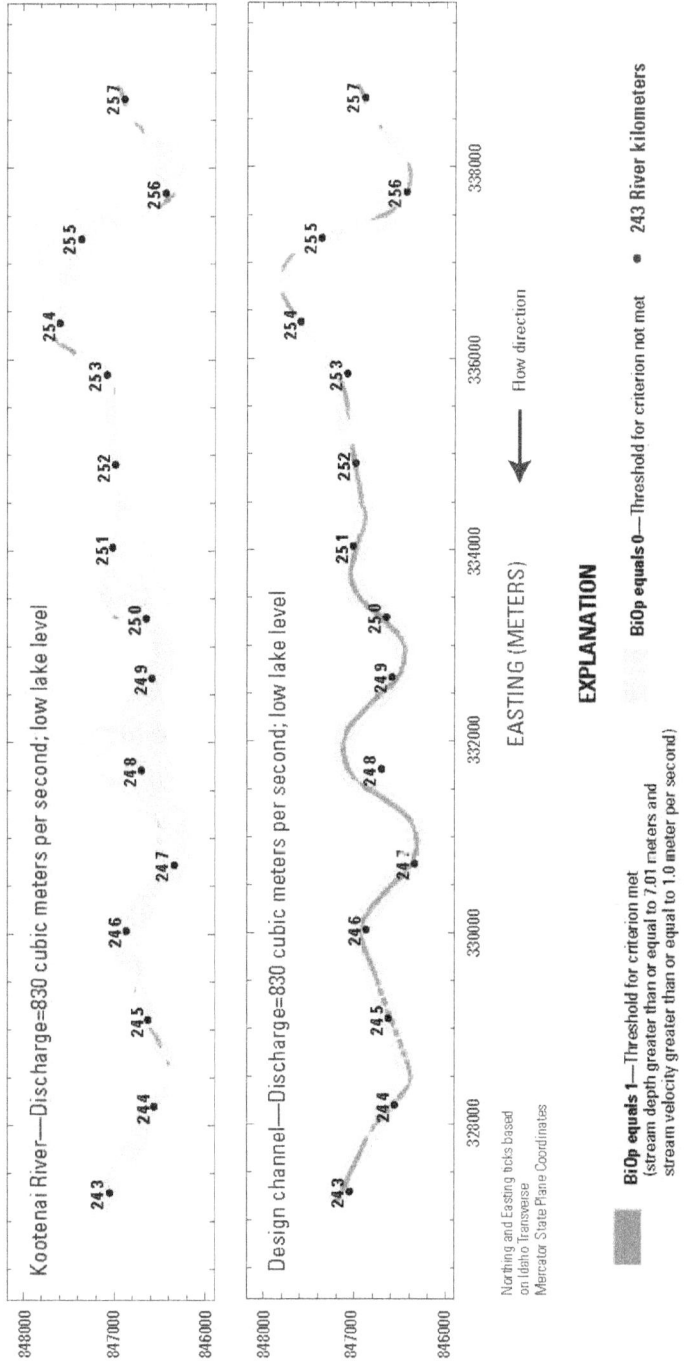

Figure 13. Graphs showing aquatic habitat suitability for the Kootenai River and the design channel based on the BiOp criterion for a discharge of 830 cubic meters per second and low Kootenay Lake level.

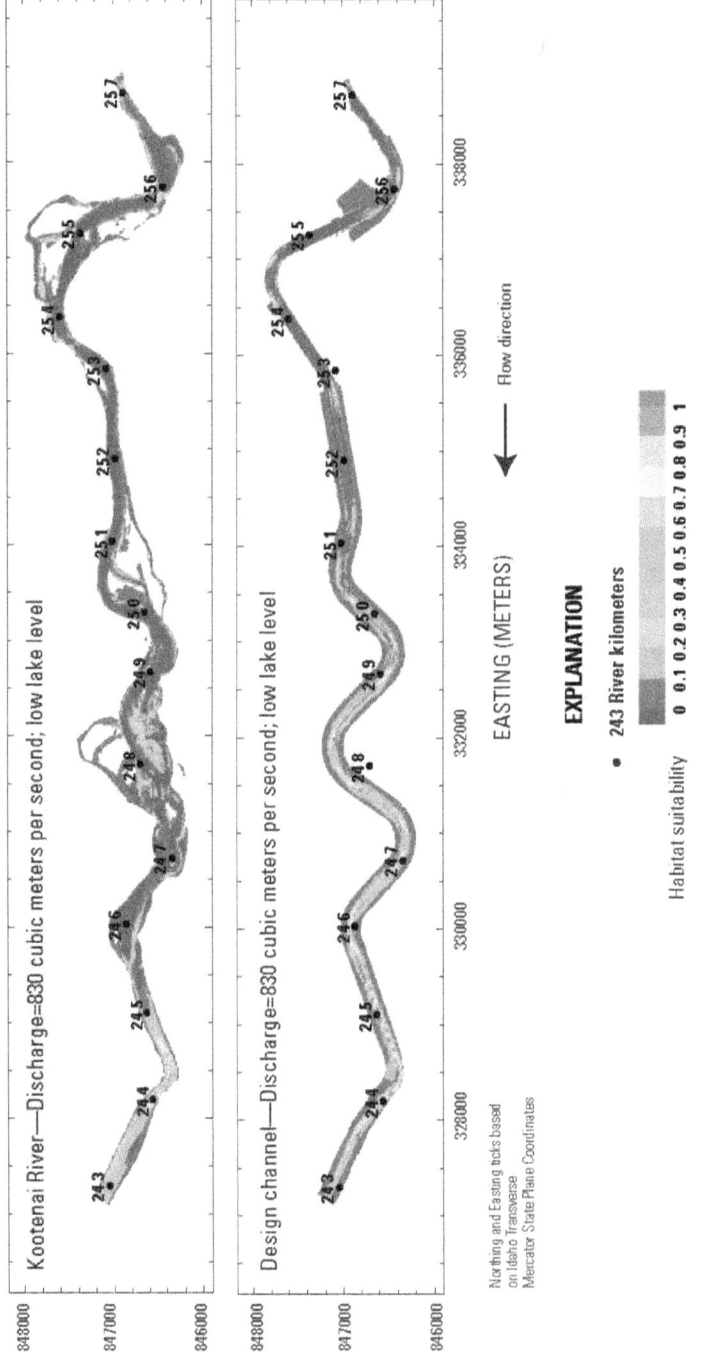

Figure 14.   Aquatic habitat suitability for the Kootenai River and the design channel based on the modeled spawning location (MSL) criterion for a discharge of 830 cubic meters per second and low Kootenay Lake level.

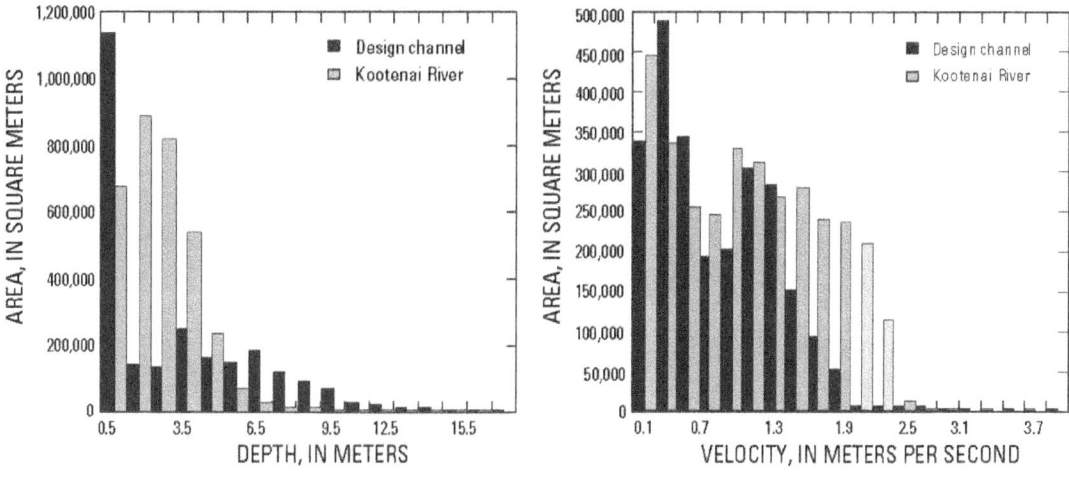

Figure 15. Stream depth and velocity in the Kootenai River and the design channel for a discharge of 830 cubic meters per second at low Kootenay Lake level.

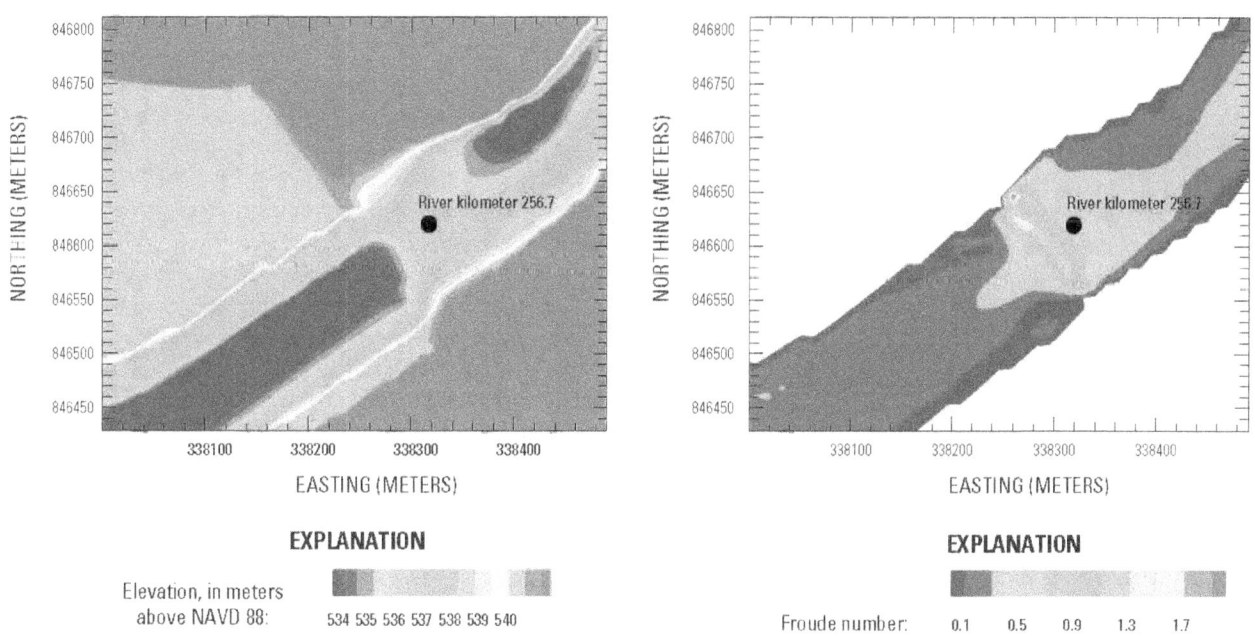

Figure 16. Channel topography and Froude number at a discharge of 555 cubic meters per second, indicating a hydraulic jump in the transition between the existing Kootenai River channel and the upstream end of the design channel.

annual load by more than an order of magnitude. Any changes to sediment supply in the system owing to installation or removal of dams or accelerated degradation or improvement of streams upstream could alter the sediment load as well.

In situations like the Kootenai River, where lake or other downstream backwater conditions are present, changes in these conditions could influence the success of the design. If the elevation of Kootenay Lake were raised, sediment transport could be reduced in the design sections of the river. If the lake were lowered, sediment transport could increase. The level of Kootenay Lake is set by an international treaty with Canada (International Joint Commission, 1938, Order of Approval, Kootenay Lake; accessed October 27, 2010, at *http://www.ijc.org/conseil_board/kootenay_lake/en/ kootenay_mandate_mandat.htm*), so either scenario is somewhat unlikely, barring unforeseen increases in flow from other tributaries to the lake or a reduction in the height of a natural control barrier to allow more hydropower generation by drawing the lake down farther. For rivers that terminate in the ocean, however, changing sea levels could cause problems with reconfigured channels.

Constructed Channel Characteristics

One of the largest unknowns for the design channel is the constructed channel roughness. Because channel roughness is based on complex interactions between the bed, banks, and sediment in the reach, the constructed channel could be rougher or smoother than anticipated. In general, a rougher channel will result in higher water-surface elevations for the same discharge than a smoother channel, which could mean more frequent inundation of the flood plain or flooding at lower discharges. A smoother channel will result in lower water-surface elevations, potentially reducing sediment transport capacity and decreasing flood-plain inundation.

The uncertainty of the design channel roughness arises because one cannot make measurements of water-surface elevations that could be used to calibrate the model. Because of this uncertainty, the ability to simulate water-surface elevations and sediment transport was tested by conducting additional experiments in a flume. These experiments demonstrate the effects of narrowing and deepening a portion of a channel, similar to the basic changes proposed in the design channel. A discussion of the flume investigations is provided in Appendix 2.

Other sources of uncertainty for the constructed channel relate to the construction methods and material used to implement the design. Larger scale projects and projects in populated areas near infrastructure clearly pose more risk. Although multidimensional modeling can provide valuable information, such as flow direction and bed stresses, additional expertise may be needed to assess the structural integrity of the design, construction feasibility, and geotechnical properties of the material used.

Additional Multidimensional Modeling Analysis

Several other tools are available in multidimensional models that could be used to further investigate design channel function and potential channel stability. These tools are not presented in this report because the preliminary Kootenai River channel design had problems that need to be addressed before further investigations are conducted. Additional modeling tools include analysis of flow vectors, which can show locations where substantial flow is directed into the bank, which may cause the bank to undercut or fail. Flow vectors can also show locations of recirculating flow, which may or may not be desirable. Other tools can model potential sediment-transport rates and erosion and deposition in a reach. These tools are currently (2010) available in the Multidimensional Surface-Water Modeling System (MD_SWMS) and could improve understanding of potential channel stability in a more complete channel design.

Summary and Conclusions

When proposed channel construction projects are large and complex, or the consequences of failure are serious, multidimensional modeling and analysis of the design channel provide insight about potential project success before the channel is built. Multidimensional models allow detailed analysis of potential water-surface levels, sediment transport, and aquatic habitat that may be created if the channel design is implemented. The method presented here stresses the need to model a range of flow conditions and potential channel roughness values to assess the designed channel for a suite of conditions. Although modeling efforts can help minimize the chance of project failure, not all variables influencing river morphology can be measured, modeled, or controlled precisely.

A preliminary channel-restoration design for the Kootenai River in northern Idaho was evaluated by the U.S. Geological Survey, in cooperation with the Kootenai Tribe of Idaho and Bonneville Power Administration, using multidimensional modeling. Simulated water-surface elevations at bankfull discharge did not match the bankfull surfaces in the design channel because boundary conditions used in the design were inconsistent with best estimates of future conditions. Channel stability analysis found that both the Kootenai River channel and the design channel are largely unable to move the D_{50} sediment through the reach at the bankfull discharge during low Kootenay Lake level. These results indicate that sediment delivered to the reach would likely be deposited in the reach, which could alter the channel geometry through time. Calculations also indicate that sand could be deposited on the flood plain of the design channel but should be transported readily through the main channel. Aquatic habitat analysis indicates that the design potentially provides more aquatic habitat suitable for spawning Kootenai River white sturgeon at lower discharges than is currently available in the river. However, the mismatch between the design flood-plain surfaces and the simulated water elevations is a serious problem that compromises the function of the channel. Problems with flood-plain function and sediment transport could potentially be alleviated if the design were substantially reworked using more appropriate lake-level boundary conditions.

Acknowledgments

The authors express their appreciation to the Kootenai Tribe of Idaho for funding this work and Sue Ireland for facilitating this project. We also thank a technical support committee composed of scientists and engineers from the Kootenai Tribe of Idaho, several local, State, and Federal agencies, and various consulting companies, including Wildland Hydrology Consultants, for their efforts reviewing and producing preliminary concept designs for the Kootenai River. Members of the U.S. Geological Survey Idaho Water Science Center collected and analyzed field data used in this report to model the Kootenai River.

References Cited

Babcock, William H., 1986, Tenmile Creek: A study of stream relocation, Water Resources Bulletin, v. 22, no. 3, p. 405–415.

Barton, G.J., Moran, E.H., and Berenbrock, Charles, 2004, Surveying cross sections of the Kootenai River between Libby Dam, Montana, and Kootenay Lake, British Columbia, Canada: U.S. Geological Survey Open-File Report 2004–1045, 35 p.

Barton, G.J., McDonald, R.R., Nelson, J.M., and Dinehart, R.L., 2005, Simulation of flow and sediment mobility using a multidimensional flow model for the white sturgeon critical-aquatic habitat reach, Kootenai River near Bonners Ferry, Idaho: U.S. Geological Survey Scientific Investigations Report 2005–5230, 54 p.

Berenbrock, Charles, 2005, Simulation of hydraulic characteristics of the white sturgeon spawning aquatic habitat of the Kootenai River near Bonners Ferry, Idaho: U.S. Geological Survey Scientific Investigations Report 2005–5110, 30 p.

Berenbrock, Charles, 2006, Simulations of hydraulic characteristics for an upstream extension of the white sturgeon spawning aquatic habitat of the Kootenai River, Idaho—A supplement to Scientific Investigations Report 2005–5110: U.S. Geological Survey Scientific Investigations Report 2006–5019, 17 p.

Berenbrock, Charles, and Bennett, J.P., 2005, Simulation of flow and sediment transport in the white sturgeon spawning aquatic habitat of the Kootenai River near Bonners Ferry, Idaho: U.S. Geological Survey Scientific Investigations Report 2005–5173, 72 p.

Copeland, R.R., McComas, D.N., Thorne, C.R., Soar, P.J., Jonas, M.M., and Fripp, J.B., 2001, Hydraulic design of stream restoration projects: U.S. Army Corps of Engineers Report ERDC/CHL TR–01–28, 175 p.

Doyle, M.W., Shields, D., Boyd, K.F., Skimore, P.B. and Dominick, D., 2007, Channel-forming discharge selection in river restoration design: Journal of Hydraulic Engineering, v. 133, no. 7, p. 831–837.

Elliott, J.G., and Capesius, J.P., 2009, Geomorphic changes resulting from floods in reconfigured gravel-bed river channels in Colorado, USA, in James, L.A., Rathburn, S.L., and Whittecar, G.R., eds., Management and restoration of fluvial systems with broad historical changes and human impacts: Boulder, Colo., Geological Society of America Special Paper 451, p. 173–198, doi: 10.1130/2009.2451(12).

Fischer, H.B., List, E.J., Koh, R.C.Y., Imberger, J., and Brooks, N.H., 1979, Mixing in inland and coastal waters: San Diego, Calif., Academic Press, 482 p.

Fosness, R.L., and Williams, M.L., 2009, Sediment characteristics and transport in the Kootenai River white sturgeon critical habitat near Bonners Ferry, Idaho: U.S. Geological Survey Scientific-Investigations Report 2009–5228, 40 p.

Frissell, C., and Nawa, R., 1992, Incidence and causes of physical failure of artificial aquatic habitat structures in streams of western Oregon and Washington: North American Journal of Fisheries Management, v. 12, p. 182–197. doi: 10.1577/1548-8675(1992)012<0182:IACOPF> 2.3.CO;2.

Hey, R.D., 2006, Fluvial geomorphological methodology for natural stable channel design: Journal of the American Water Resources Association, v. 42, no. 2, p. 357–374.

Kondolf, G.M., and Micheli, E.R., 1995, Evaluating stream restoration projects: Environmental Management, v. 19, no. 1, p. 1–15.

Kondolf, G.M., Smeltzer, M.W., and Railsback, S.R., 2001, Design and performance of a channel reconstruction project in a coastal California gravel-bed stream: Environmental Management, v. 28, no. 6, p.761–776.

Kootenai Tribe of Idaho, 2009, Kootenai River habitat restoration project master plan—A conceptual feasibility analysis and design framework: Bonners Ferry, Idaho.

McDonald, R.R., Nelson, J.M., Paragamian, V., Barton, G.J., 2010, Modeling the effect of flow and sediment transport on white sturgeon spawning habitat on the Kootenai River, Idaho: Journal of Hydraulic Engineering, v. 136, no. 12, p. 1077–1092.

McDonald, R.R., Bennett, J.P., and Nelson, J.M., 2001, The USGS multi-dimensional surface water modeling system, in Proceedings of the Federal Interagency Sedimentation Conference, 7th, Reno, Nev., March 21–25, 2001: Reno, Nev., Subcommittee on Sedimentation, p. I-161–I-167.

McDonald, R.R., Nelson, J.M., Kinzel, P.J., and Conaway, J., 2006, Modeling surface-water flow and sediment mobility with the Multi-Dimensional Surface Water Modeling System (MD_SWMS): U.S. Geological Survey Fact Sheet 2005–3078, 4 p.

Middleton, G.V., and Southard, J.B., 1984, Mechanics of sediment movement: Society of Economic Paleontologists and Mineralogists, Short Course 3, 401 p.

Moerke, A.H., and Lamberti, G.A., 2004, Restoring stream ecosystems—Lessons from a Midwestern State: Restoration Ecology, v. 12, no. 3, p. 327–334.

Nelson, J.M., Bennett, J.P., and Wiele, S.M., 2003, Flow and sediment transport modeling, *in* Kondolph, G.M., and Piegay, H., eds., Tools in fluvial geomorphology: Chichester, England, Wiley and Sons, p. 539–576.

Nelson, J.M., and McDonald, R.R., 1996, Mechanics and modeling of flow and bed evolution in lateral separation eddies: U.S. Geological Survey Director's approved report submitted to the USGS Grand Canyon Monitoring and Research Center and available at *http://www.gcmrc.gov/library/reports/GCES/Physical/hydrology/Nelson1996.pdf*.

Nelson, J.M., McLean, S.R., and Wolfe, S.R., 1993, Mean flow and turbulence fields over two-dimensional bedforms: Water Resources Research, v. 29, p. 3935–3953.

Palmer, M.A., Bernhared, E.S., Alla, J.D., Lake, P.S., Alexander, G., Brooks, S., Carr, J., Clayton, S., Dahm, C.N., Follstad Shah, J., Galat, D.L., Loss, S.G., Goodwin, P., Hart, D.D., Hassett, B., Jenkinson, R., Kondolf, G.M., Lave, R., Meyer, J.L., O'Donnel, T.K., Pagano, L., and Sudduth, E., 2005, Standards for ecologically successful river restoration: Journal of Applied Ecology, v. 42, p. 208–217.

Paragamian, V.L., Beamesderfer, R.C., and Ireland, S.C., 2005, Status, population dynamics, and future prospects of the endangered Kootenai River white sturgeon population with and without hatchery intervention—Spawning locations and movement of Kootenai River white sturgeon: Transactions of the American Fisheries Society, v. 134, 14 p.

Parker, G., Toro-Escobar, C.M., Ramey, M., and Beck, S., 2003, The effect of floodwater extraction on the morphology of mountain streams: Journal of Hydraulic Engineering, v. 129, no. 11, p. 885–895.

Rosgen, D.L., 1996, The natural channel design method for river restoration, American Society of Civil Engineers Conference Proceedings, 1996, DOI:10.1061/40856(200)344.

Rouse, H., 1937, Modern conceptions of the mechanics of turbulence: Transactions of the American Society of Civil Engineers, v. 102, p. 463–543.

Shields, F.D., Copeland, R.R., Klingeman, P.C., Doyle, M.W., and Simon, A., 2003, Design for stream restoration: Journal of Hydraulic Engineering, v. 129 no. 8, p. 575–584.

Smith, S.M., and Prestegaard, K.L., 2005, Hydraulic performance of a morphology-based stream channel design: Water Resources Research, v. 41, W11413, doi:10.1029/2004WR003926.

Tompkins, M.R., and Kondolf, G.M., 2007, Systematic post-project appraisals to maximize lessons learned from river restoration projects: case study of compound channel restoration projects in northern California: Restoration Ecology, v. 15, no. 3, p. 524–537.

U.S. Fish and Wildlife Service, 1994, Endangered and threatened wildlife and plants; determination of endangered status for the Kootenai River population of white sturgeon—Final rule: Federal Register, v. 59, no. 171, p. 45989–46002.

U.S. Fish and Wildlife Service, 1999, Recovery plan for the Kootenai River population of the white sturgeon (*Acipenser transmontanus*): Portland, Oreg., U.S. Fish and Wildlife Service [variously paged].

U.S. Fish and Wildlife Service, 2006, Fish and Wildlife Service Biological Opinion regarding The effects of Libby Dam operations on the Kootenai River white sturgeon, bull trout, and kootenai sturgeon critical aquatic habitat: Portland, Oreg., document number 1–9–01–F–0279R, 167 p.

U.S. Fish and Wildlife Service, 2008, Critical aquatic habitat revised designation for the Kootenai River population of the white sturgeon (*Acipenser transmontanus*)—Final rule: Federal Register, v. 73, no. 132, p. 39506–39523.

Waddle, T.J., ed., 2001, PHABSIM for Windows—User's manual and exercises: U.S. Geological Survey Open-File Report 2001–340, 288 p.

Wohl, E., Angermeier, P.L., Bledsoe, B., Kondolf, G.M., MacDonnell, L., Merritt, D.M., Palmer, M.A., Poff, N.L., and Tarbonton, D., 2005, River restoration: Water Resources Research, v. 41, W10301, doi:10.1029/2005WR003985.

Wolman, M.G., and Miller, W.P., 1960, Magnitude and frequency of forces in geomorphic processes: Journal of Geology, v. 68, no. 1, p. 54–74.

Appendix 1: Maps of Simulated Stream Depth, Stream Velocity, Shear Stress, Rouse Number, and Aquatic Habitat in the Kootenai River and the Design Channel

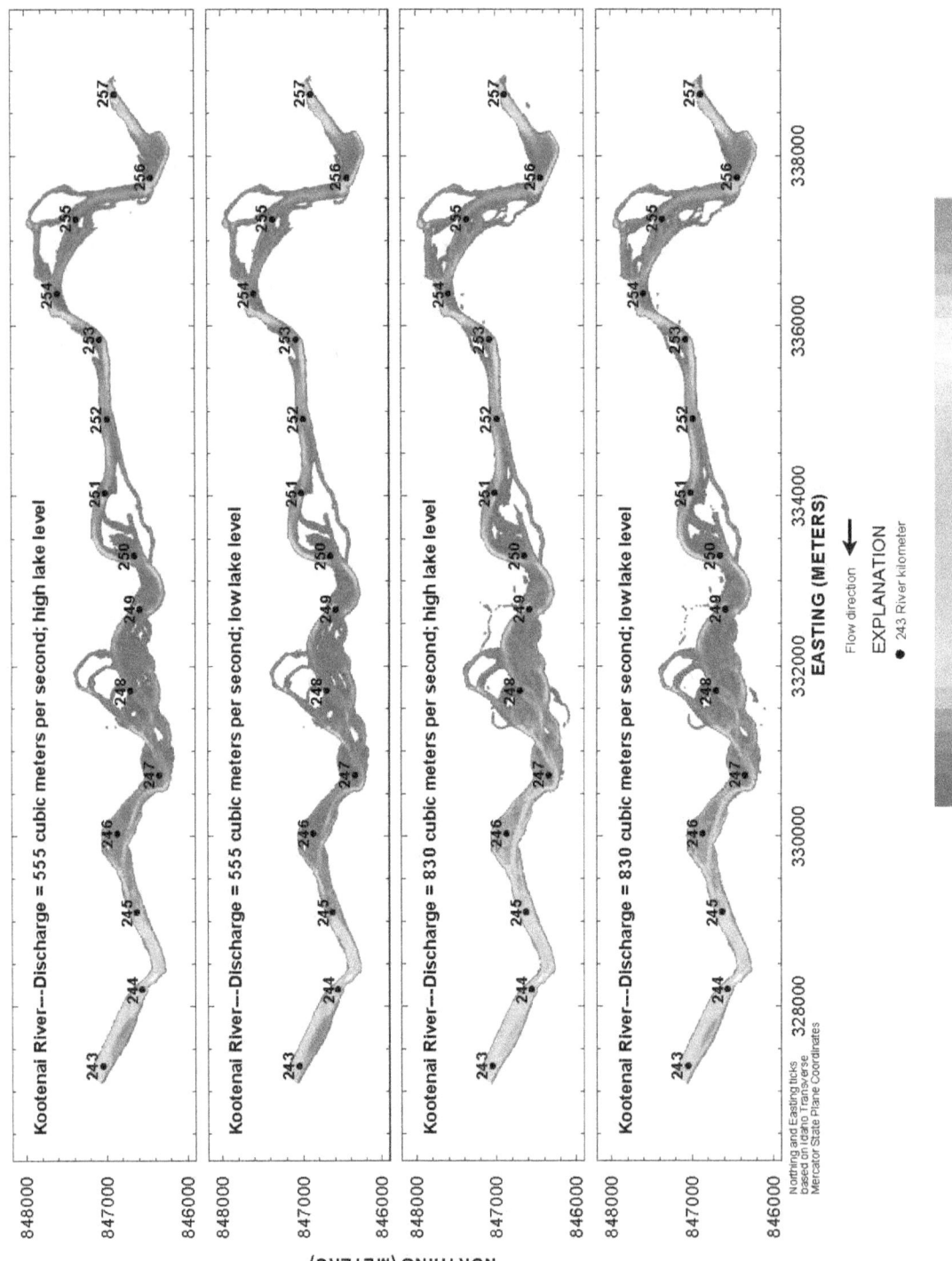

Figure 1–1.   Simulated stream depth for the Kootenai River and the design channel for all discharges and lake levels.

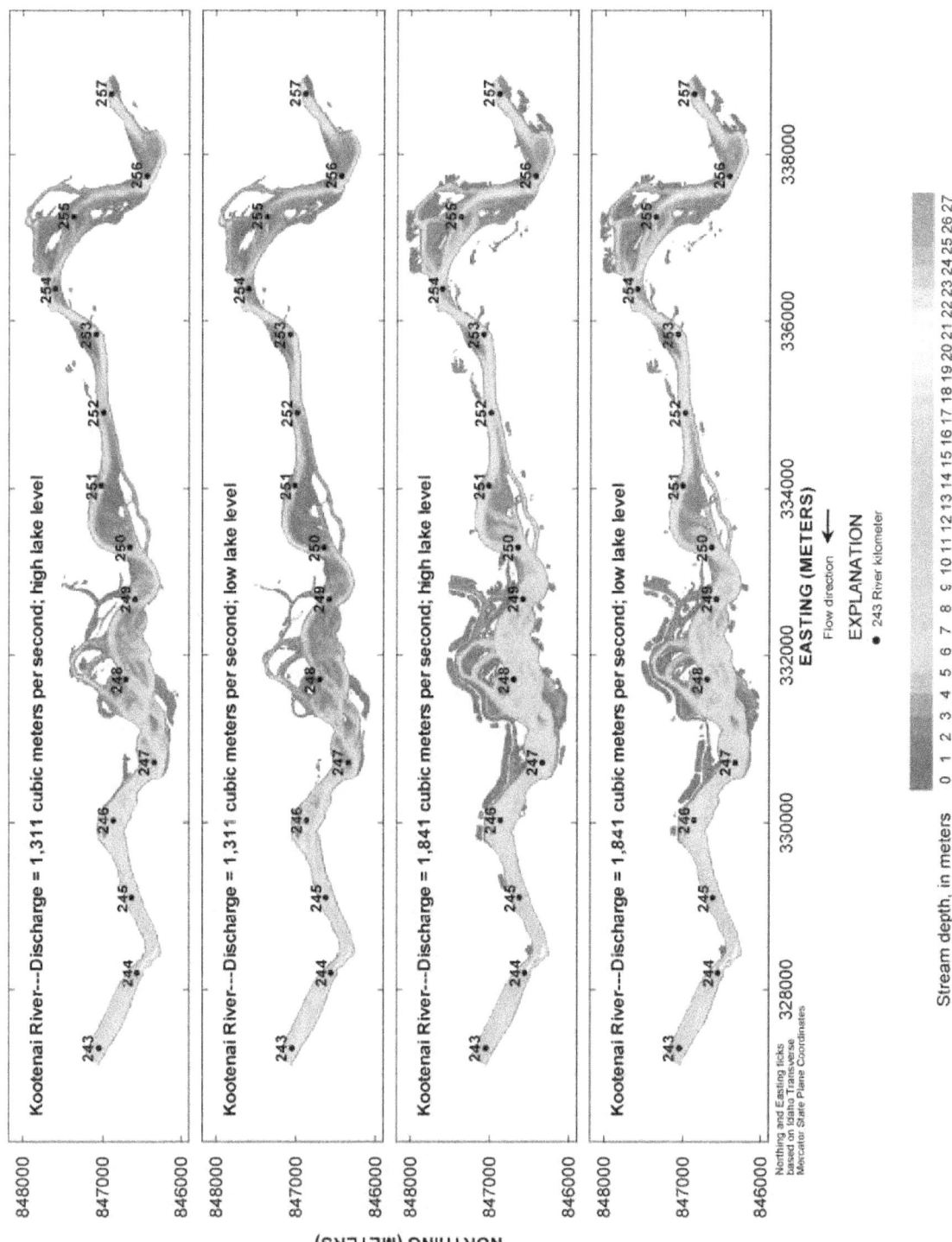

Figure 1-1. Simulated stream depth for the Kootenai River and the design channel for all discharges and lake levels.—Continued

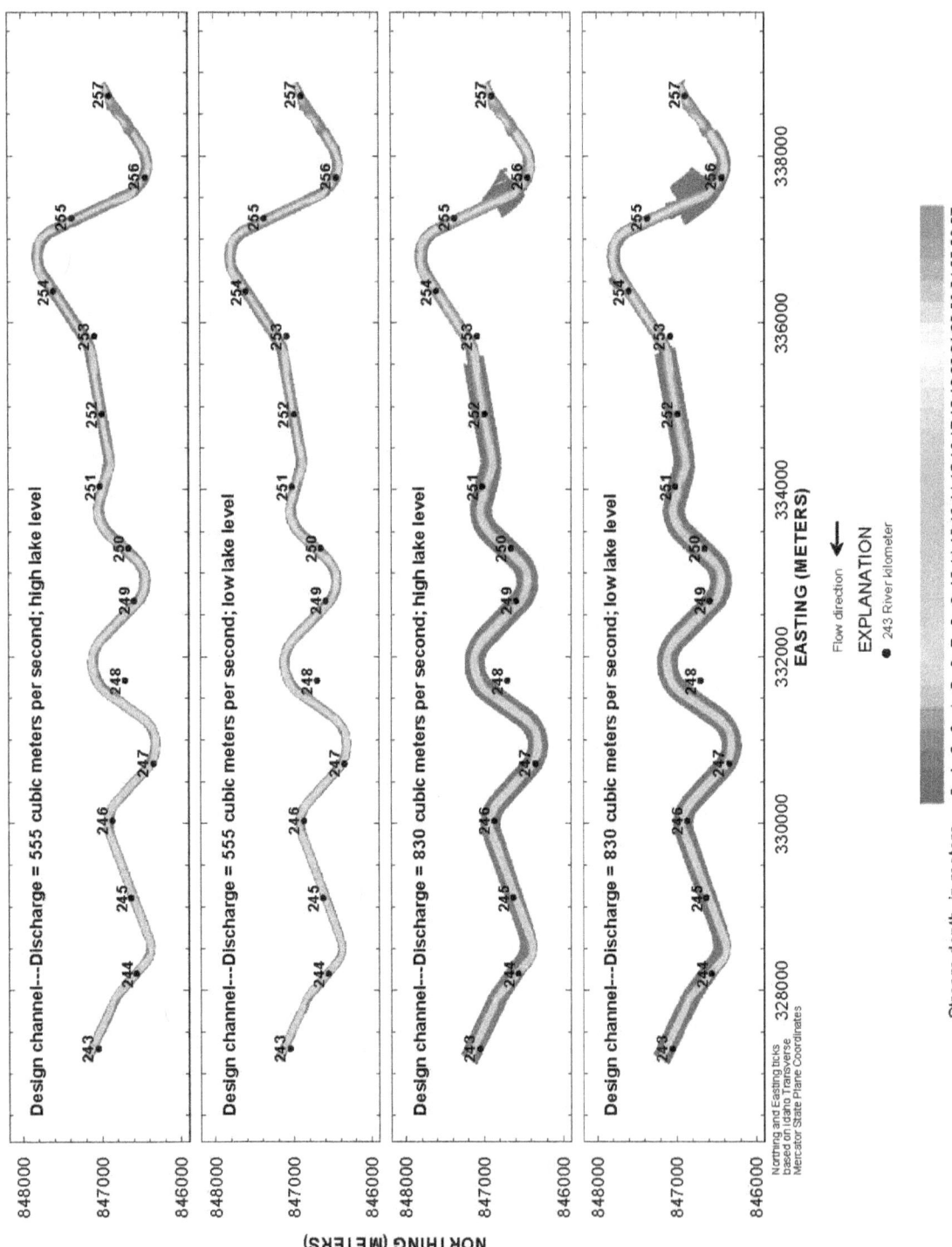

Figure 1–1.   Simulated stream depth for the Kootenai River and the design channel for all discharges and lake levels.—Continued

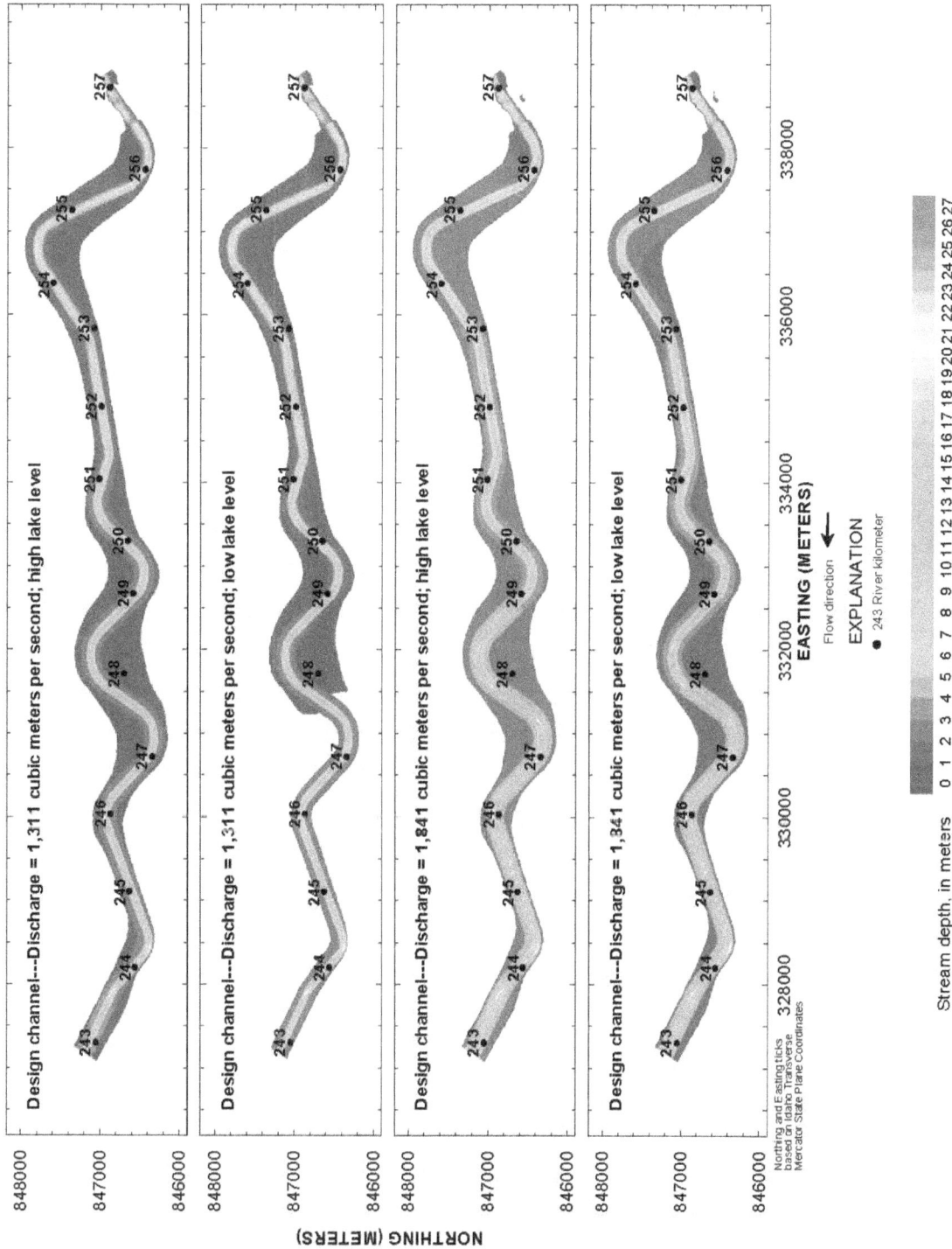

Figure 1–1. Simulated stream depth for the Kootenai River and the design channel for all discharges and lake levels.—Continued

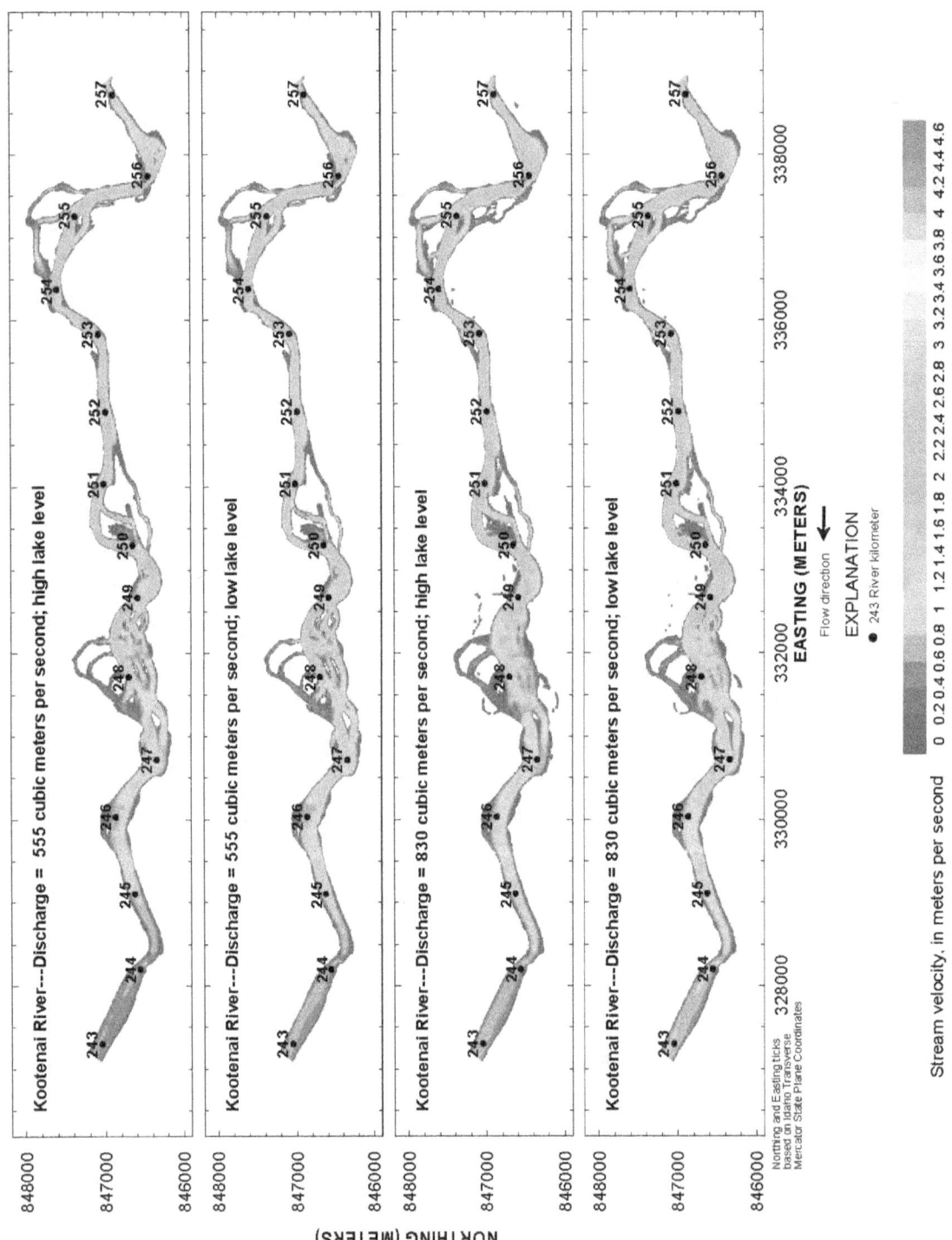

Figure 1–2. Simulated stream velocity for the Kootenai River and the design channel for all discharges and lake levels.

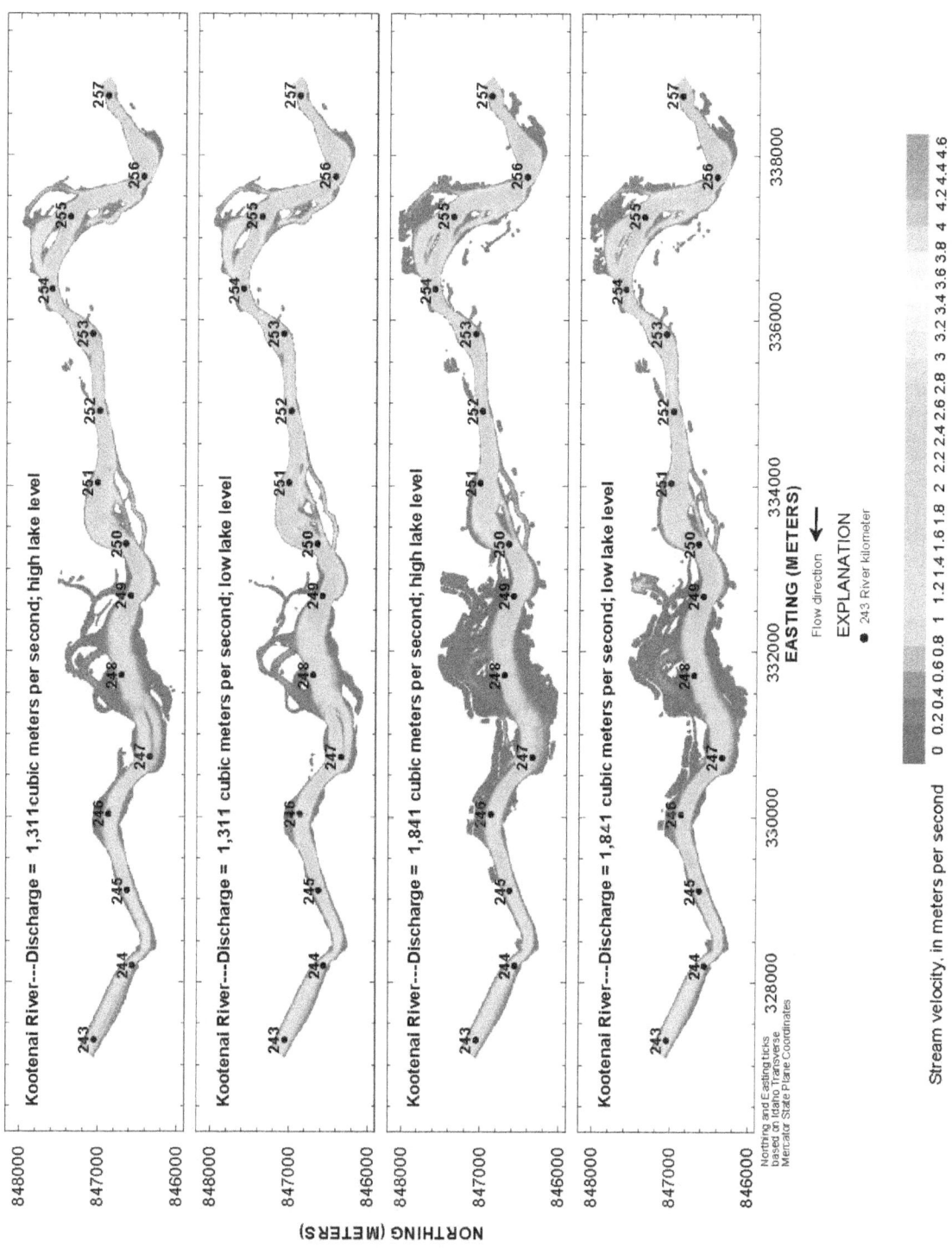

Figure 1-2. Simulated stream velocity for the Kootenai River and the design channel for all discharges and lake levels.—Continued

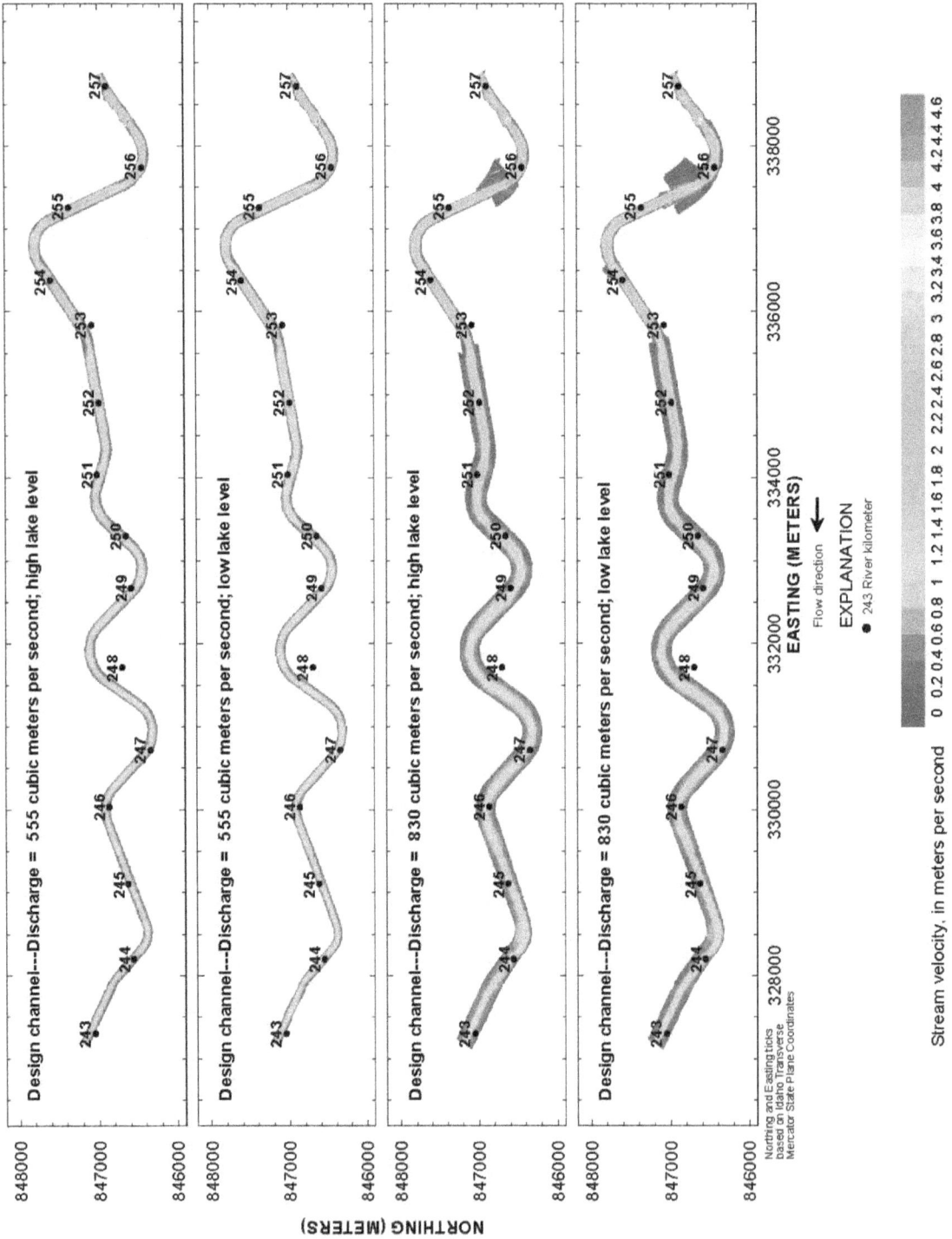

Figure 1–2. Simulated stream velocity for the Kootenai River and the design channel for all discharges and lake levels.—Continued

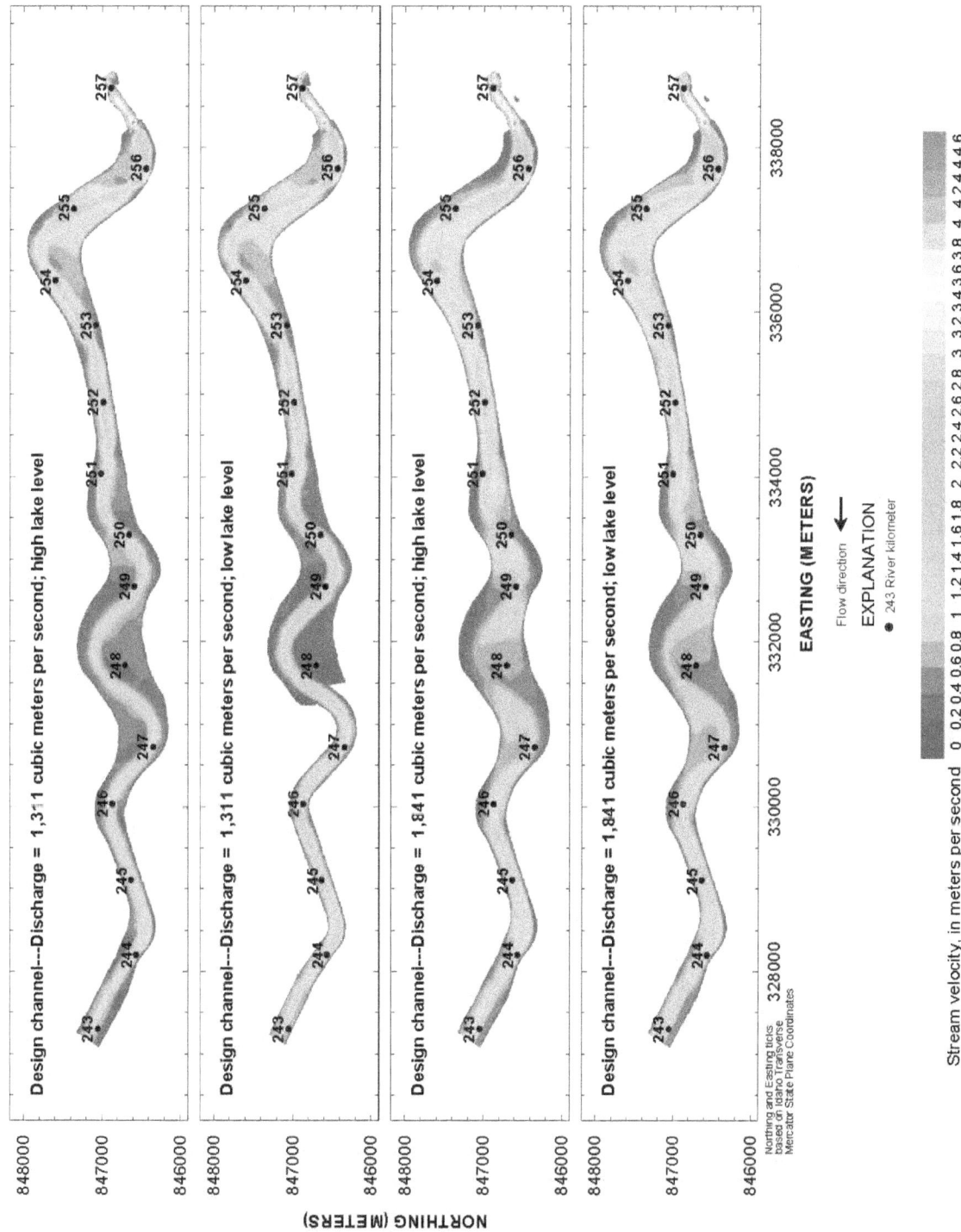

Figure 1–2. Simulated stream velocity for the Kootenai River and the design channel for all discharges and lake levels.—Continued

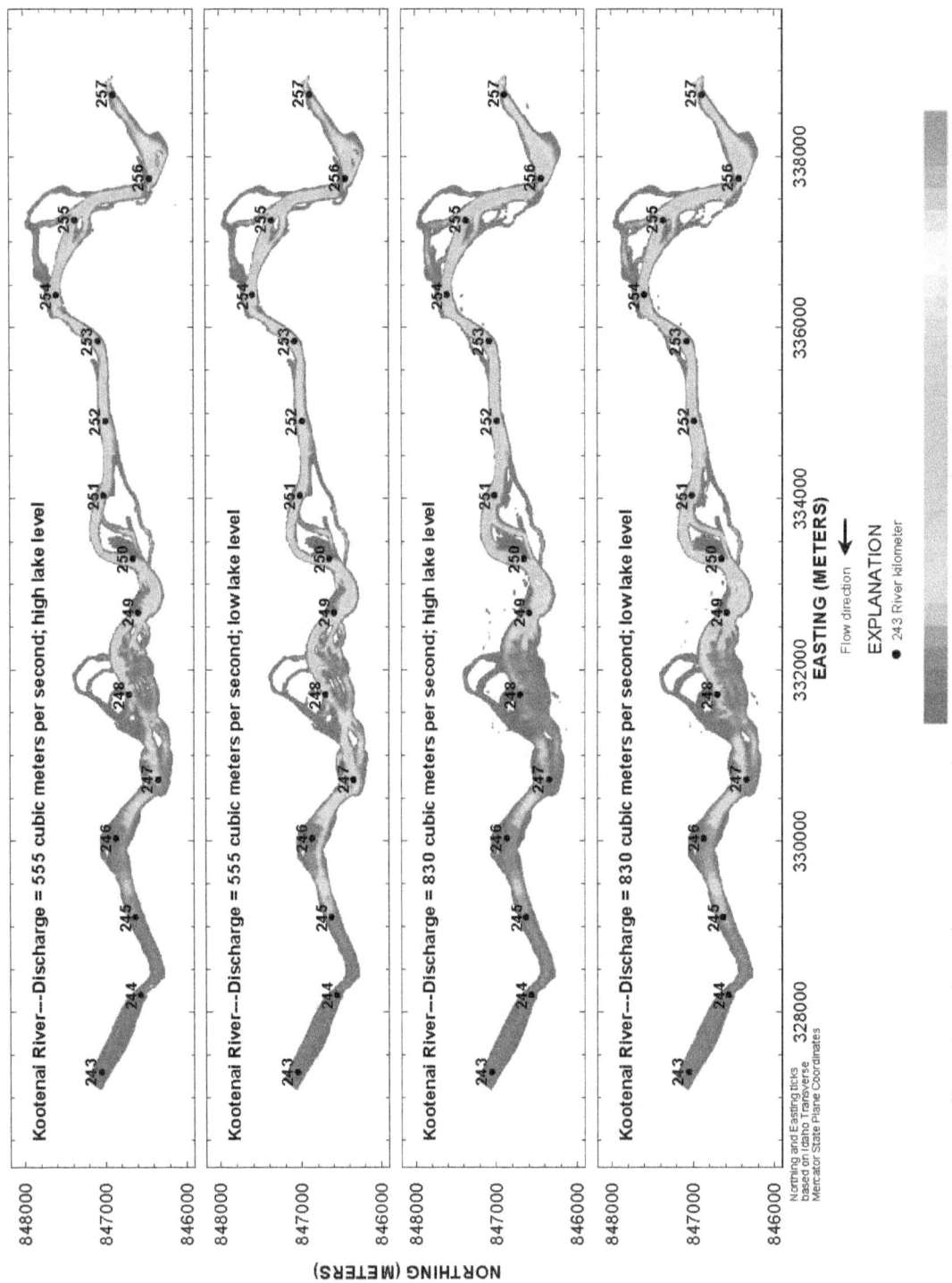

Figure 1–3.   Simulated shear stress for the Kootenai River and the design channel for all discharges and lake levels.

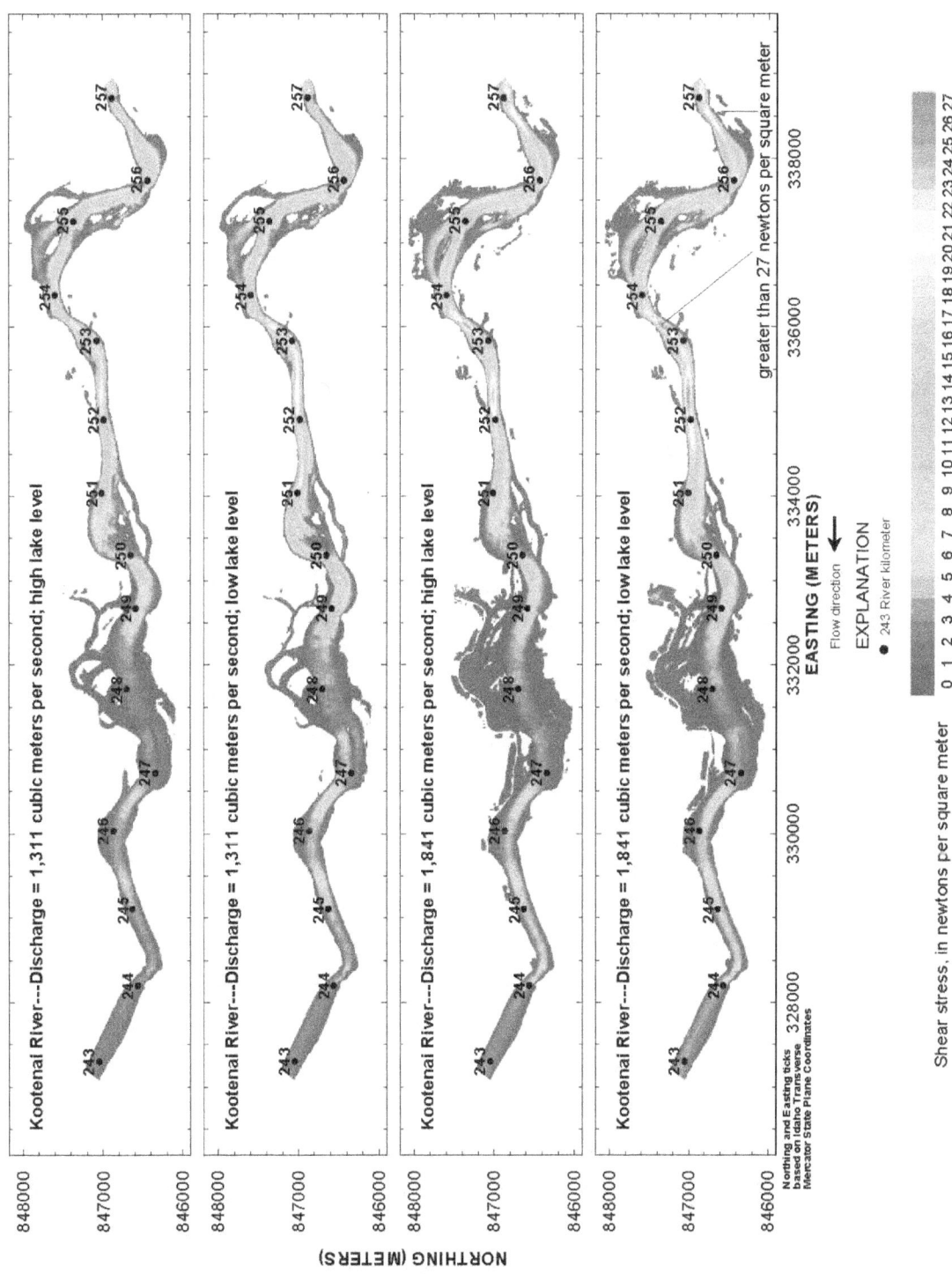

Figure 1–3. Simulated shear stress for the Kootenai River and the design channel for all discharges and lake levels.—Continued

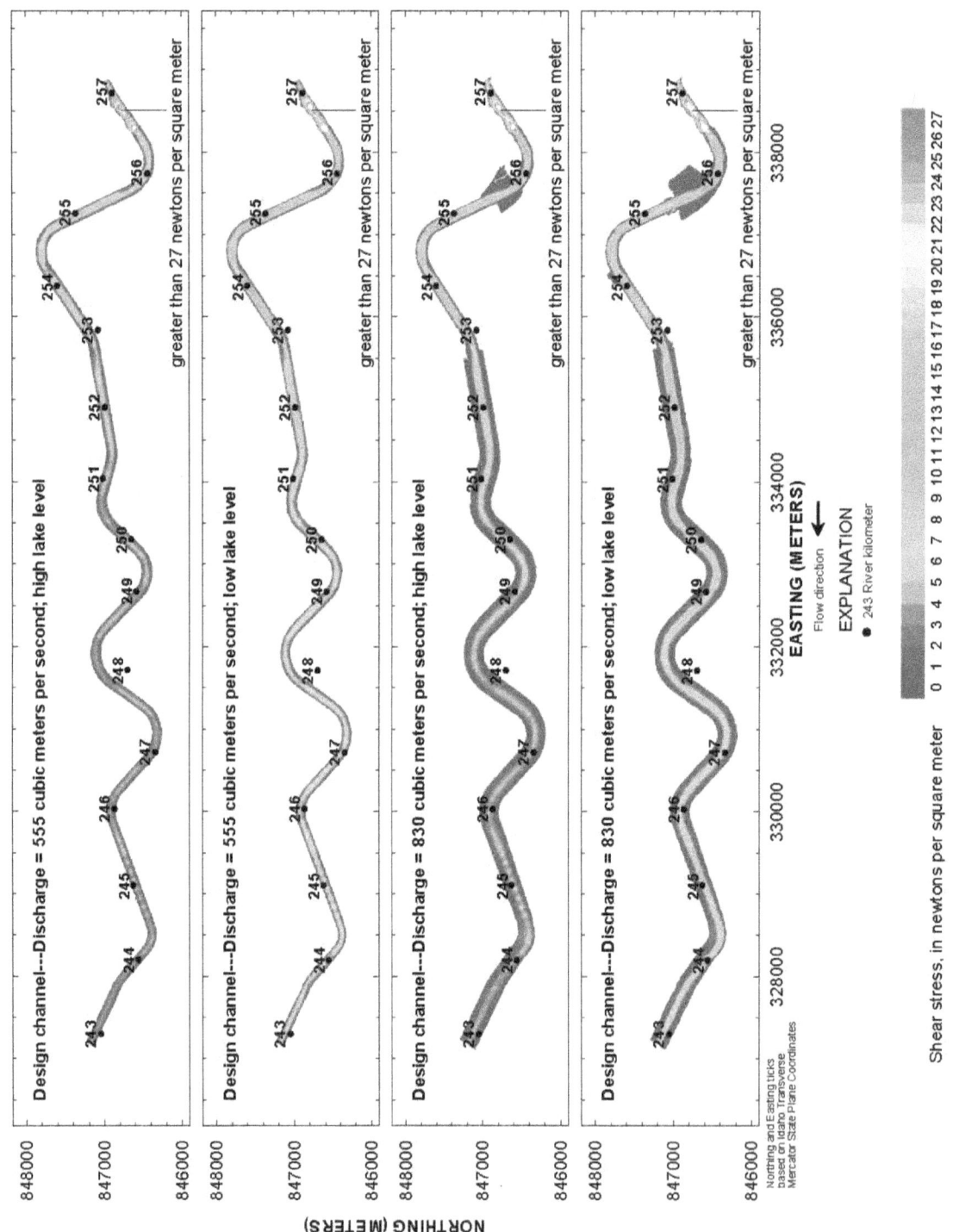

Figure 1–3. Simulated shear stress for the Kootenai River and the design channel for all discharges and lake levels.—Continued

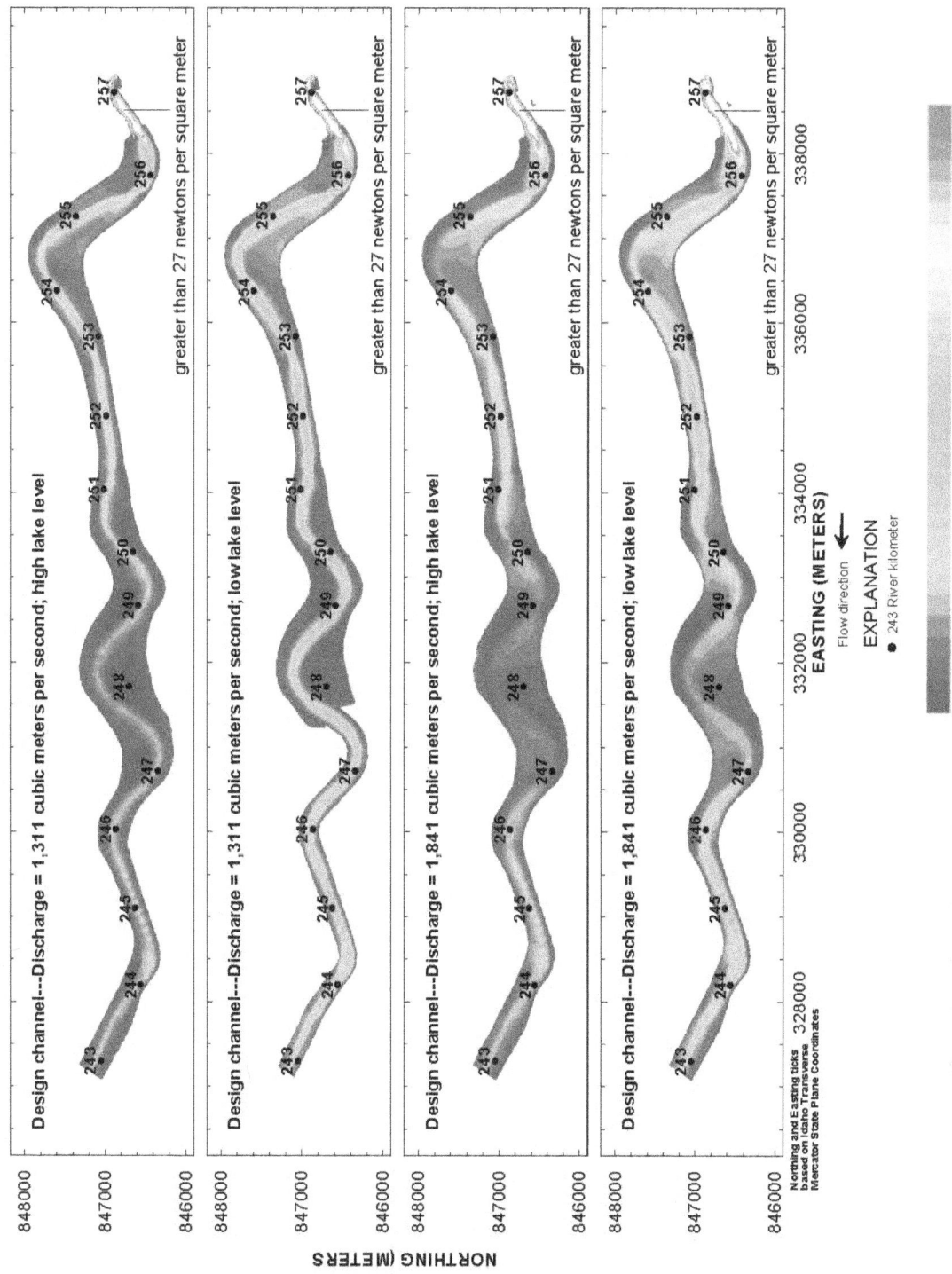

Figure 1–3. Simulated shear stress for the Kootenai River and the design channel for all discharges and lake levels.—Continued

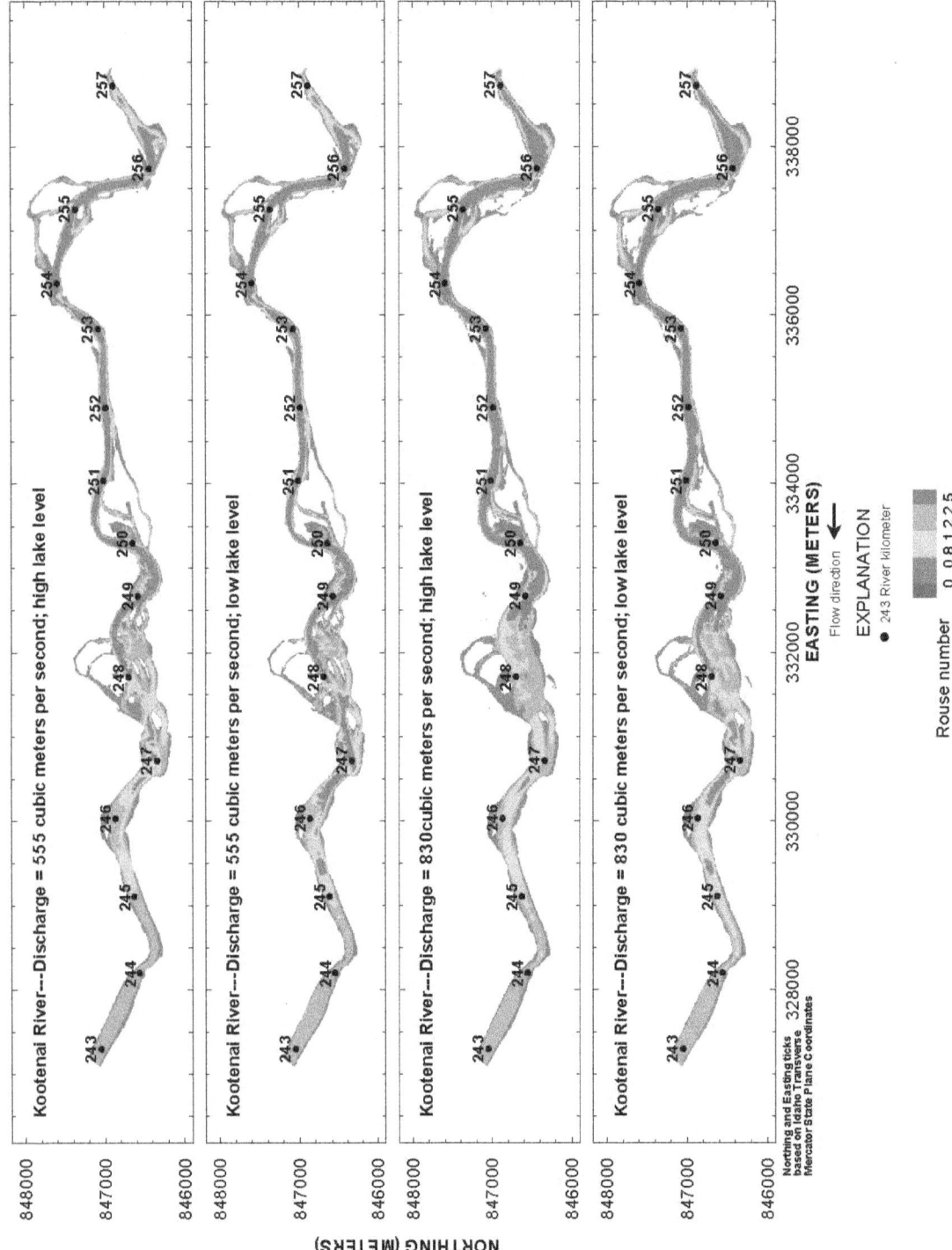

Figure 1–4. Model-calculated Rouse number for the Kootenai River and the design channel for all simulated discharges and lake levels. Rouse number calculations used a grain size of 0.023 centimeter.

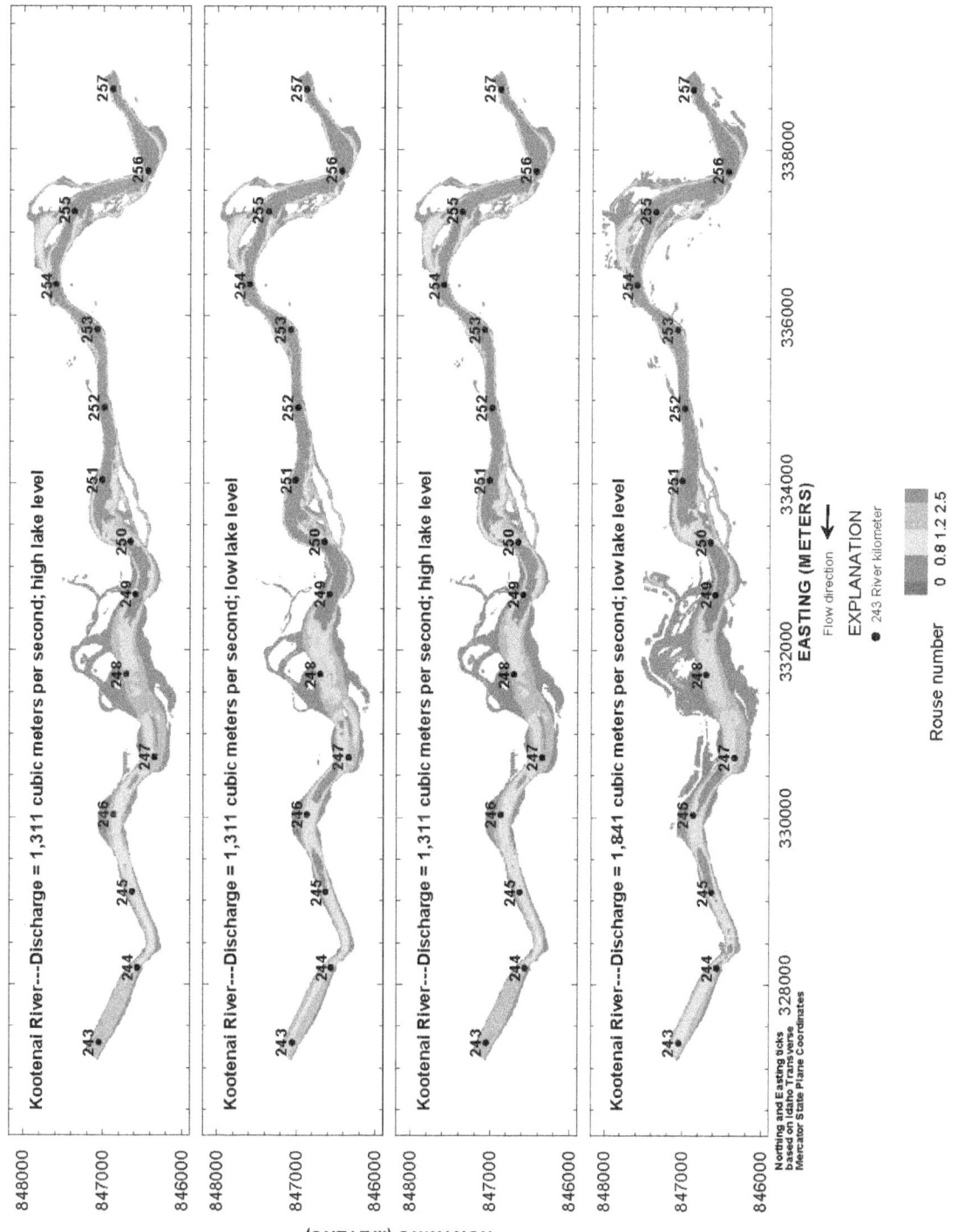

Figure 1–4.   Model-calculated Rouse number for the Kootenai River and the design channel for all simulated discharges and lake levels. Rouse number calculations used a grain size of 0.023 centimeter.—Continued

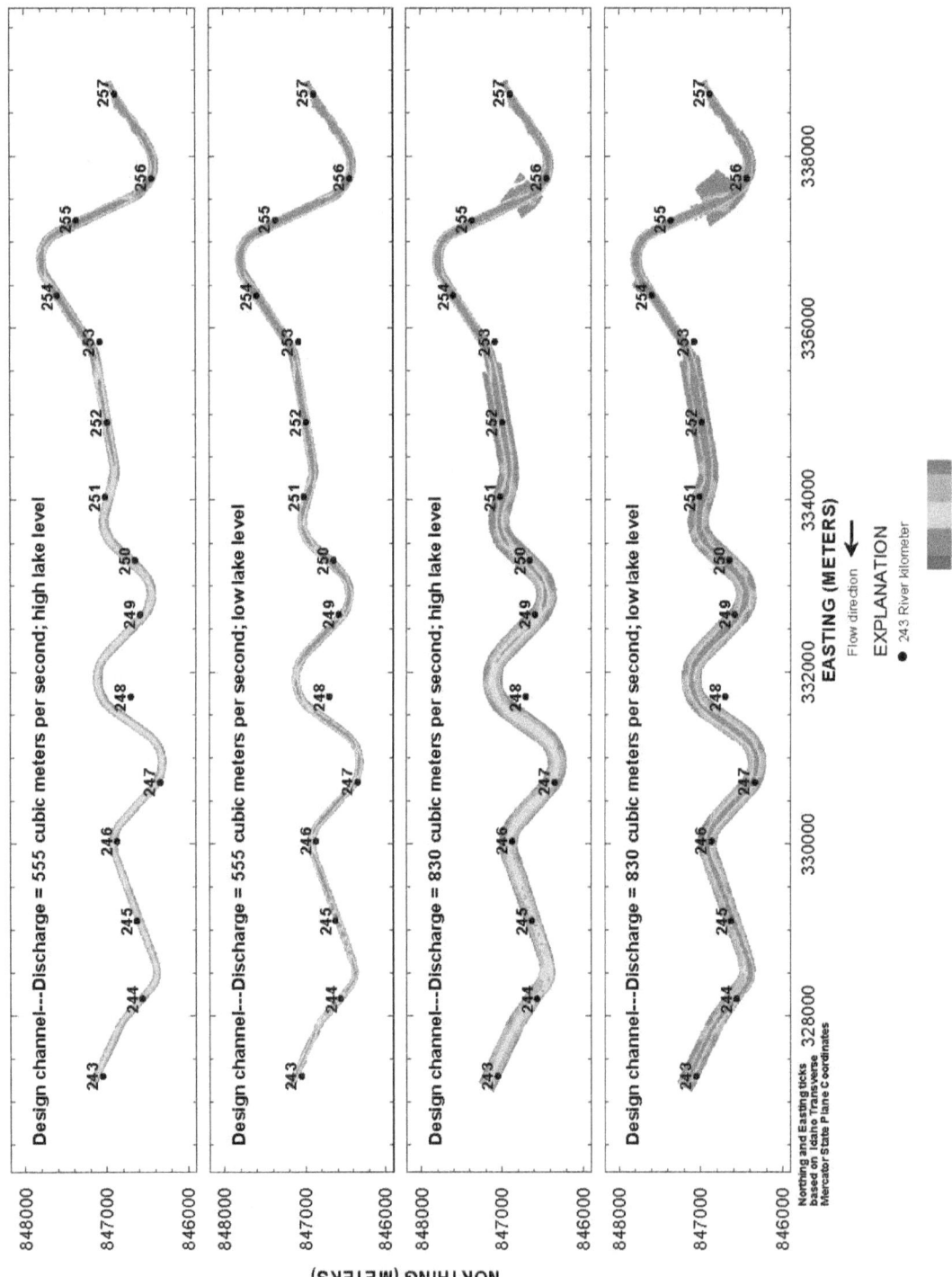

Figure 1–4. Model-calculated Rouse number for the Kootenai River and the design channel for all simulated discharges and lake levels. Rouse number calculations used a grain size of 0.023 centimeter.—Continued

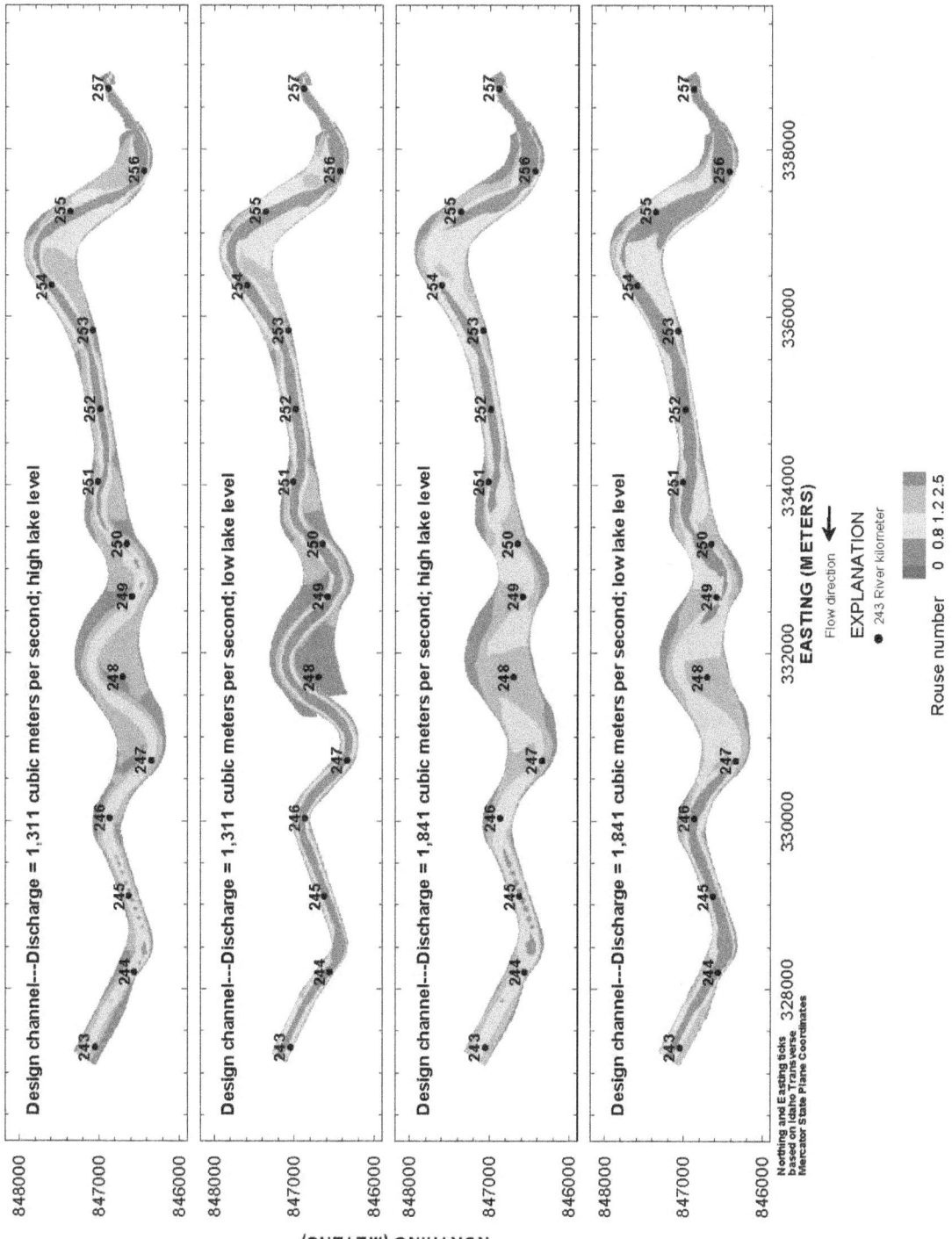

Figure 1–4. Model-calculated Rouse number for the Kootenai River and the design channel for all simulated discharges and lake levels. Rouse number calculations used a grain size of 0.023 centimeter.—Continued

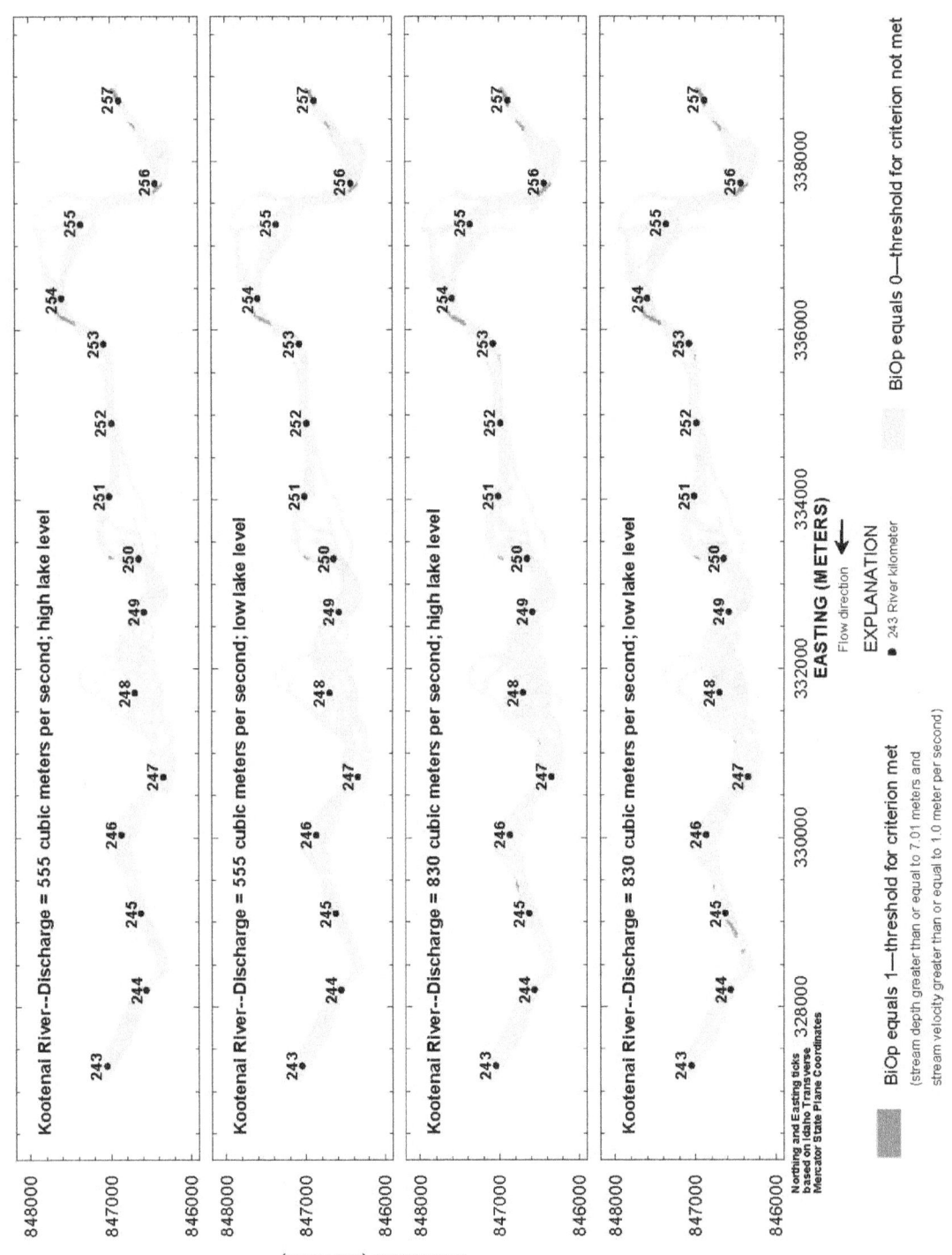

Figure 1–5. Aquatic habitat suitability for the Kootenai River and the design channel based on the BiOp criterion for all simulated discharges and lake levels.

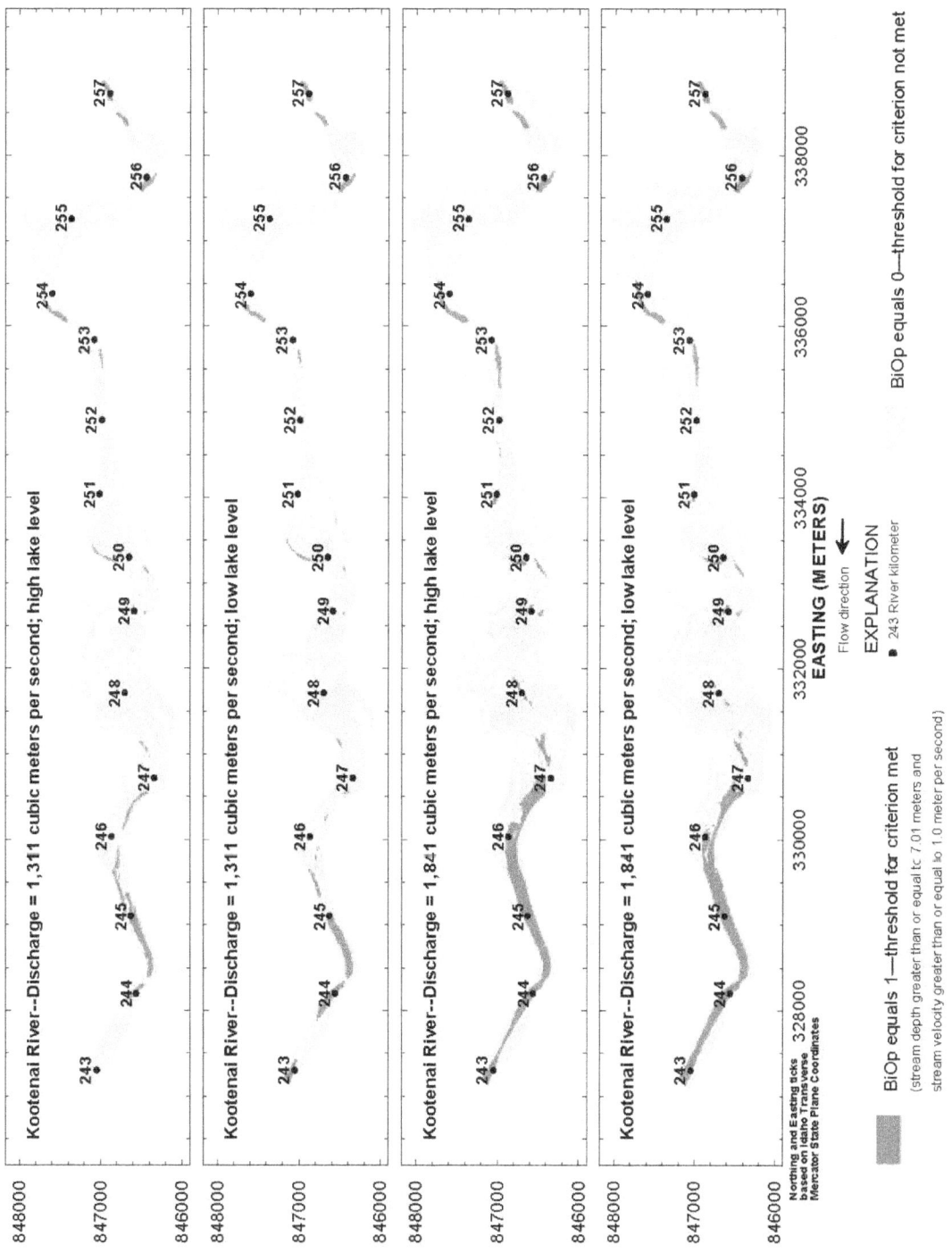

Figure 1-5. Aquatic habitat suitability for the Kootenai River and the design channel based on the BiOp criterion for all simulated discharges and lake levels.—Continued

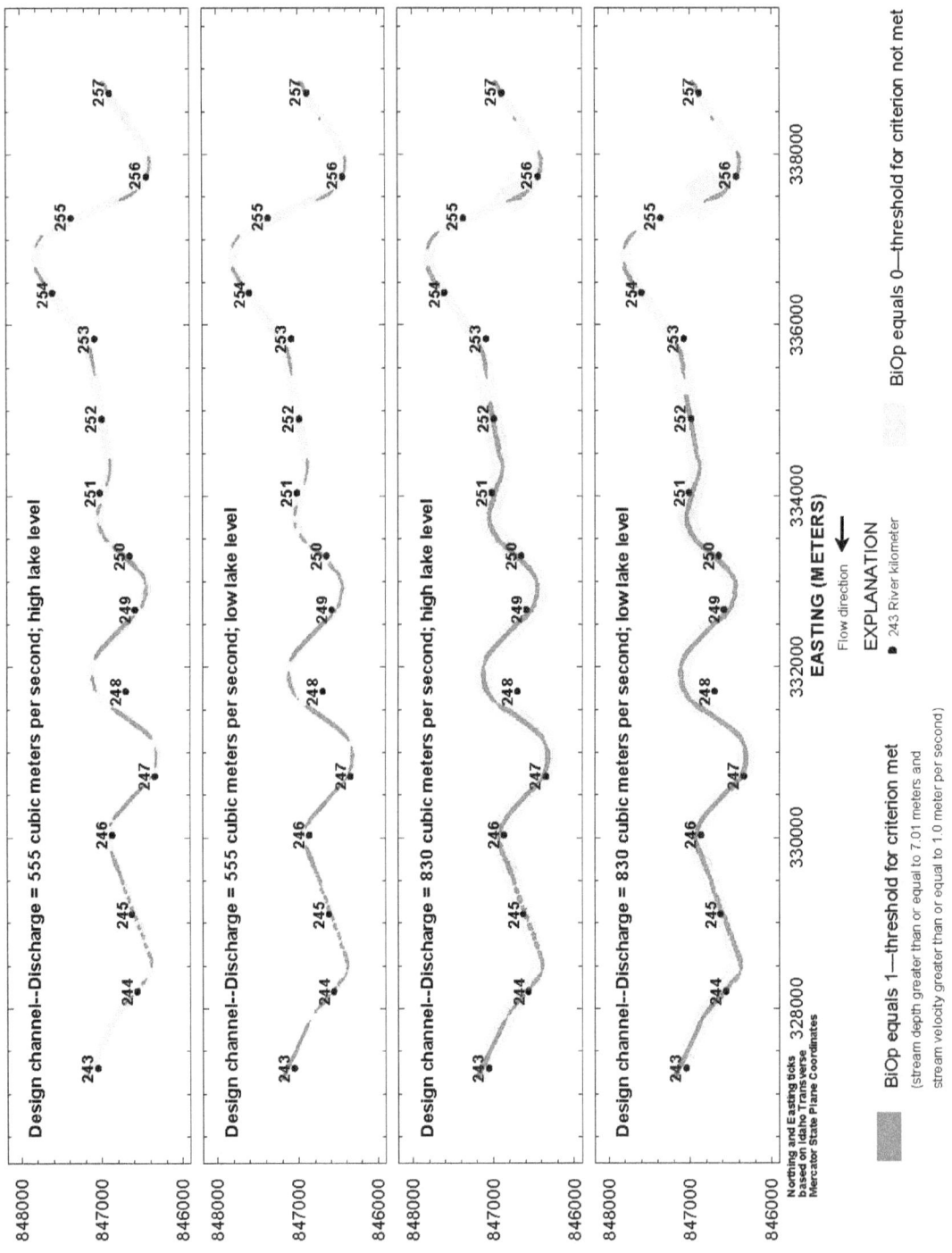

Figure 1–5. Aquatic habitat suitability for the Kootenai River and the design channel based on the BiOp criterion for all simulated discharges and lake levels.—Continued

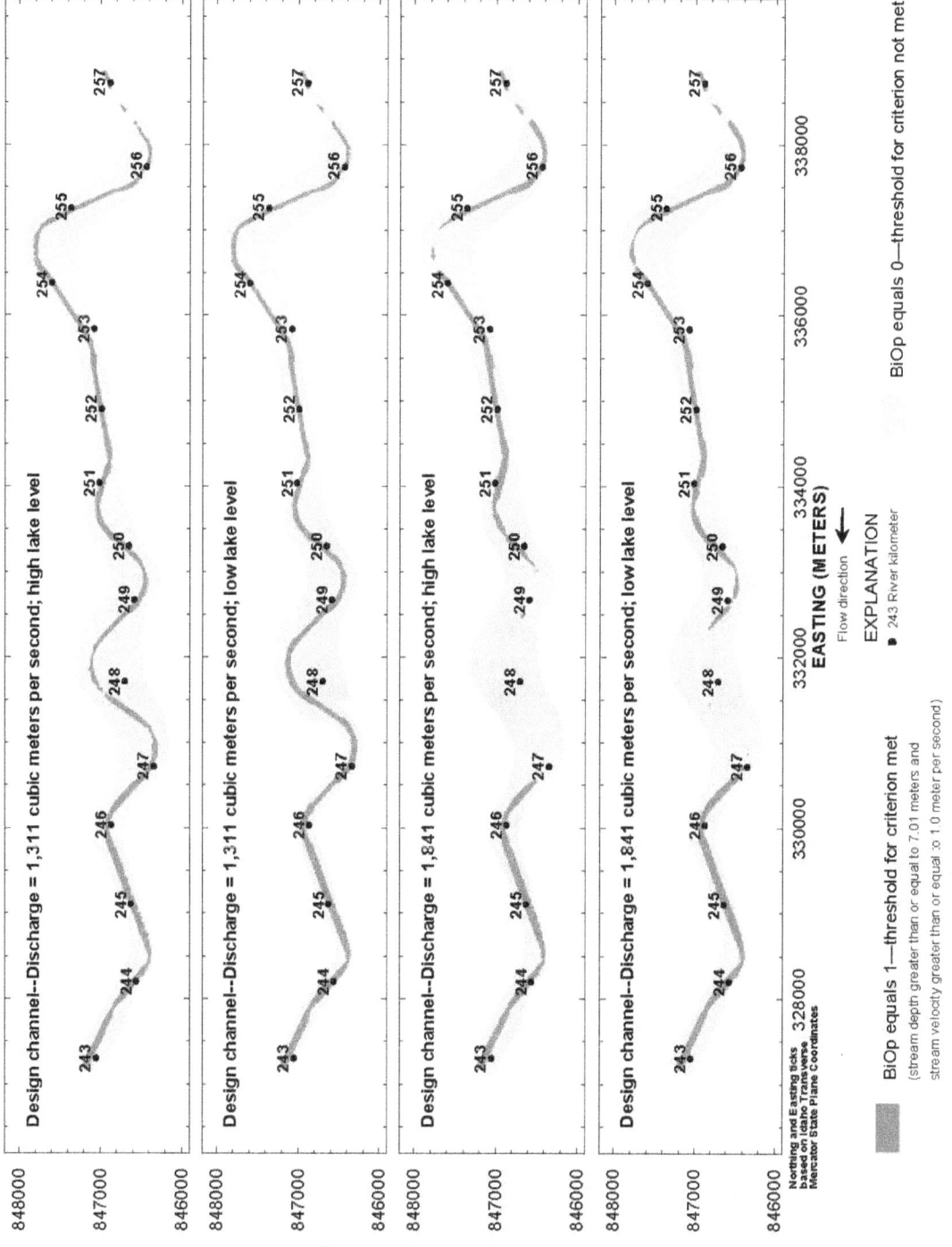

Figure 1–5. Aquatic habitat suitability for the Kootenai River and the design channel based on the BiOp criterion for all simulated discharges and lake levels.—Continued

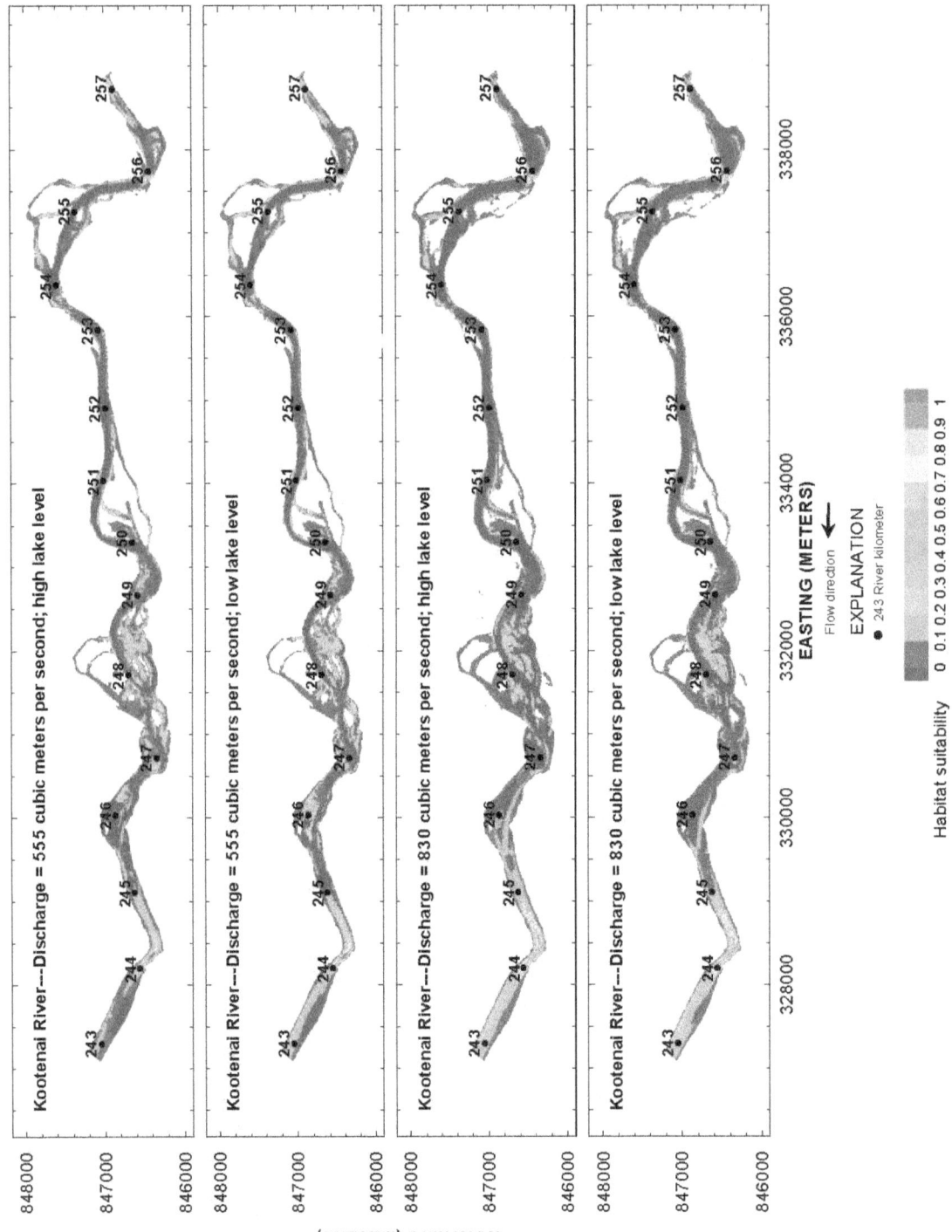

Figure 1–6.   Aquatic habitat suitability for the Kootenai River and the design channel based on the modeled spawning location (MSL) criterion for all simulated discharges and lake levels.

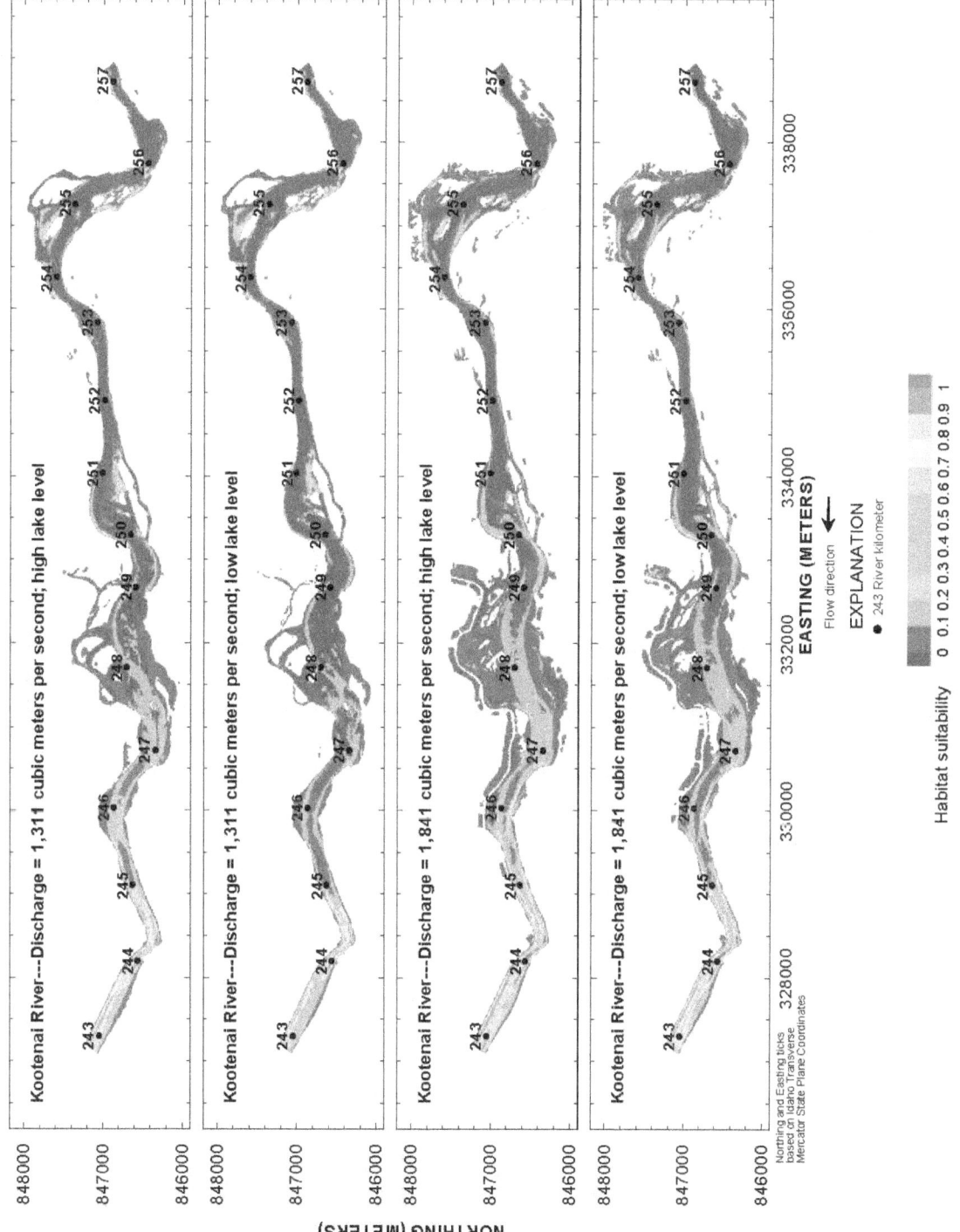

Figure 1-6. Aquatic habitat suitability for the Kootenai River and the design channel based on the modeled spawning location (MSL) criterion for all simulated discharges and lake levels.—Continued

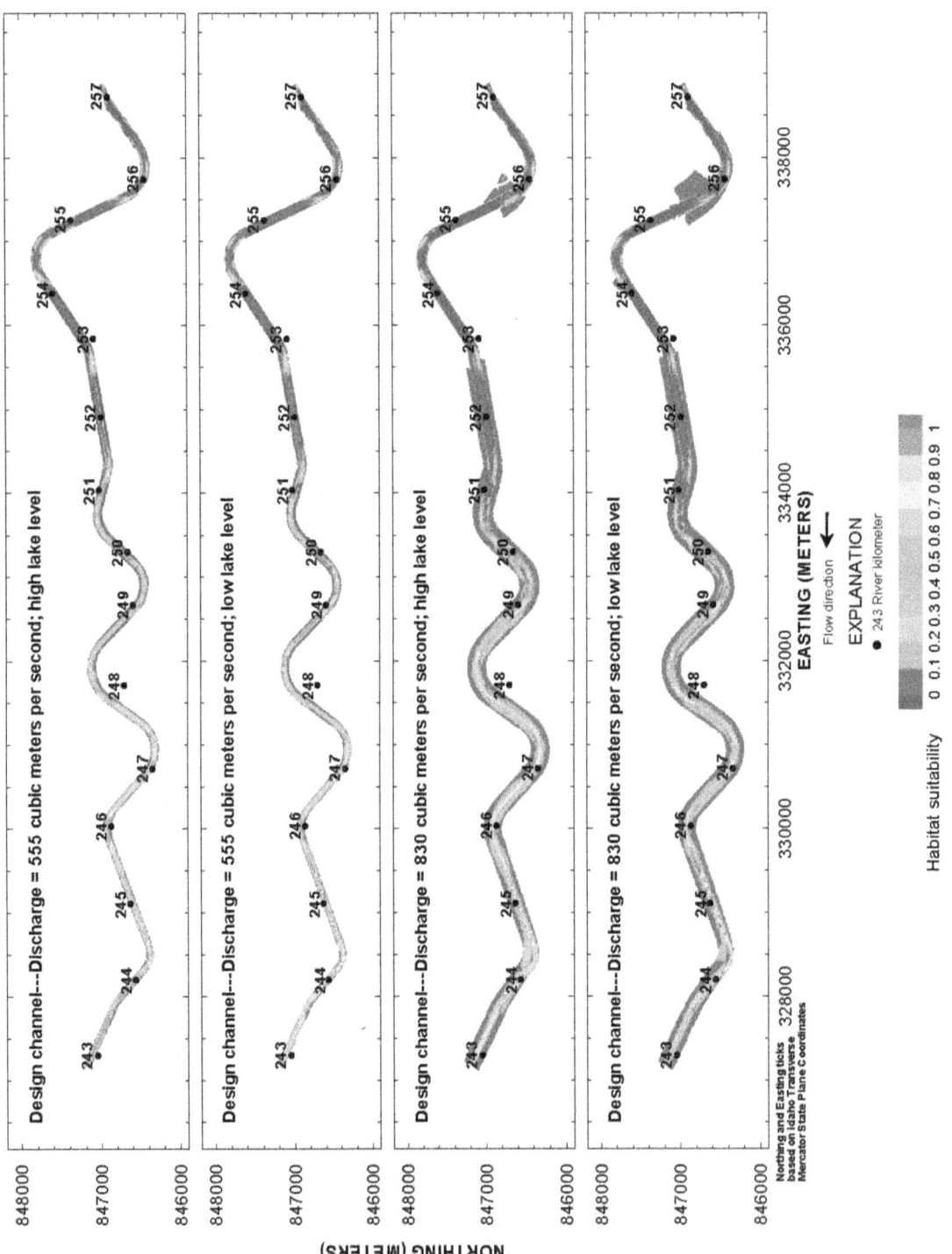

Figure 1-6. Aquatic habitat suitability for the Kootenai River and the design channel based on the modeled spawning location (MSL) criterion for all simulated discharges and lake levels.—Continued

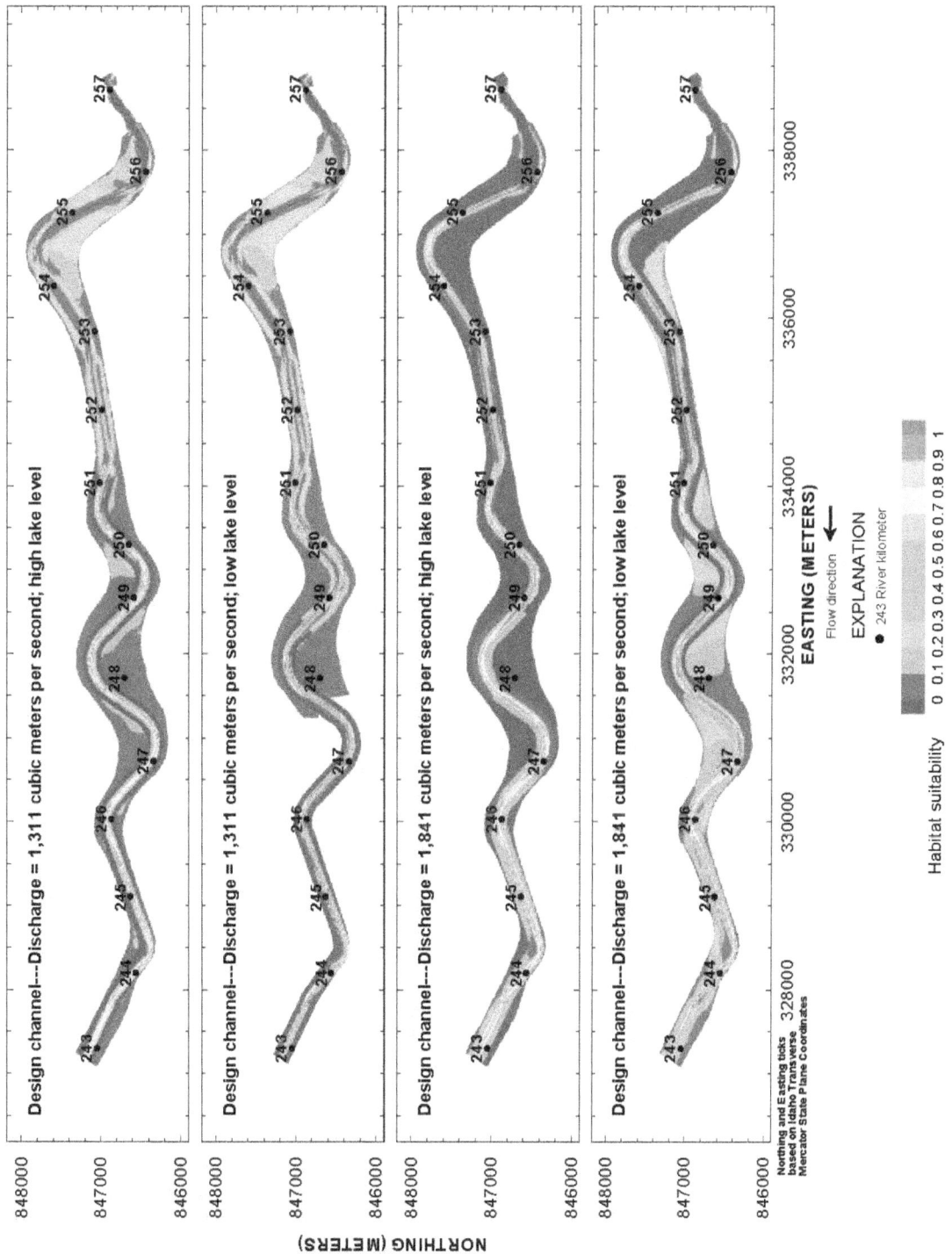

Figure 1–6. Aquatic habitat suitability for the Kootenai River and the design channel based on the modeled spawning location (MSL) criterion for all simulated discharges and lake levels.—Continued

Appendix 2: Flume Investigations

Purpose

Channel restoration has been proposed on the Kootenai River in northern Idaho to provide improved spawning habitat for the endangered Kootenai River white sturgeon. One proposed channel design would transform a naturally quasi-braided reach of the river into a single-thread channel that is much narrower and deeper in order to provide improved stream depths, stream velocity, and substrate for sturgeon habitat. However, the Kootenai River in this area is fairly complex, containing an abrupt transition from the steeper quasi-braided reach to an extremely low gradient meander reach that is strongly influenced by backwater conditions. Due to the complexity of the system and the unusually large scale of the proposed design, there is concern about how altering this system will change sediment transport and patterns of erosion and deposition, which could affect the overall stability of the river or alter conditions near infrastructure, such as the bridge on U.S. Highway 95 (at RKM 245.9, fig. 2). Because of these concerns, multidimensional modeling was used to simulate the proposed channel design to evaluate potential water-surface elevations, sediment transport, and aquatic habitat. However, many measurements typically required by flow models to constrain boundary conditions and(or) to calibrate the flow model were unavailable given that measurements cannot be made of a channel that does not yet exist. Therefore, flume investigations were conducted in an effort to test the modeling approach by simulating flow for two experimental flume channels.

Testing the modeling approach involved conducting flume experiments and simulating the flume channels by using measurements made during the experiments. Two experimental channels were created that demonstrated some of the proposed channel changes in the channel design. Channel 1 was configured to reproduce key sediment transport characteristics of the existing Kootenai River. Channel 2 was altered to test the effects of narrowing and deepening the upper one-third of channel 1, which at a very basic level is the primary change proposed by the design channel. Two discharges were used in each flume channel to determine the effects of moderate and high discharges. During each discharge experiment, observations of sediment transport and transport mode were made. The bed of the flume channels also was surveyed before and after each experiment to assess locations of erosion and deposition. These measurements were used to model the flume scenarios in the Multidimensional Surface-Water Modeling System (MD_SWMS) (McDonald and others, 2001; McDonald and others, 2006). This allowed us to test our ability to simulate water-surface elevations and sediment-transport processes, which were components of the multidimensional evaluation of the design channel. In addition, the flume work provides an opportunity to better understand how different channel configurations and discharges may affect sediment transport.

Flume Methodology

The flume used in these experiments is 7.31 m long and 1.25 m wide. It is equipped with a camera and laser mounted on a traverse that can be used to accurately survey the topography of the channel and the water surface to within ±0.002 m. The survey equipment operates over most of the flume, from 0.7 m downstream from the head gate to 0.6 m upstream from the outlet. The survey system measures a 6-m-long section of the flume at cross sections spaced every 0.1 m and cross-section points every 0.01 m. Controllable valves allow discharges of approximately 1 liter per second (L/s) to 15 L/s and can be programmed to generate variable or essentially steady discharge.

The primary objective in developing the flume channels was to reproduce the essential sediment-transport processes in the Kootenai River. The most important process is transport of gravel, which shapes channel morphology and maintains channel geometry. Gravel-size sediment in the braided reach of the Kootenai River is immobile at a moderate discharge of 500 m³/s and only sporadically mobile at higher discharges such as 1,300 m³/s. Channel 1 was configured such that it was incapable of transporting a flume sediment corresponding to gravel at a moderate discharge of approximately 3 L/s and capable of transporting the sediment at a corresponding high discharge of approximately 12 L/s.

Both flume channels were formulated to be very simple compared to the Kootenai River or the design channel. No attempt was made to reproduce the sinuosity or complex channel geometry of those channels. The flume channels had straight vertical walls and rectangular channel geometry. Both channels were divided into three segments: the upper one-third represented conditions in the braided reach, the middle one-third represented the straight reach, and the lower one-third represented the meander reach (fig. 2–1).

Channel 1 was developed by adjusting the width, depth, slope, and sediment size in a set of calculations that determined whether or not a given sediment size could be transported at 3 L/s in each reach (table 2–1). Once a suitable channel was determined, the same calculations were performed for the higher discharge to ensure that the sediment would be mobile at that flow. The width/depth ratios of the actual Kootenai River could not be maintained without allowing the Froude number to rise above critical. For this reason, the width/depth ratios in the flume were substantially larger than those in the actual channel, but the ratios were held at reasonable values for braided and meandering channel morphology in the respective reaches. The resulting channel was therefore not a strict physical or Froude scale model. It also was not possible to exactly scale the Kootenai River channel because of limitations in scaling gravel and fine sand in the Kootenai River down to flume size.

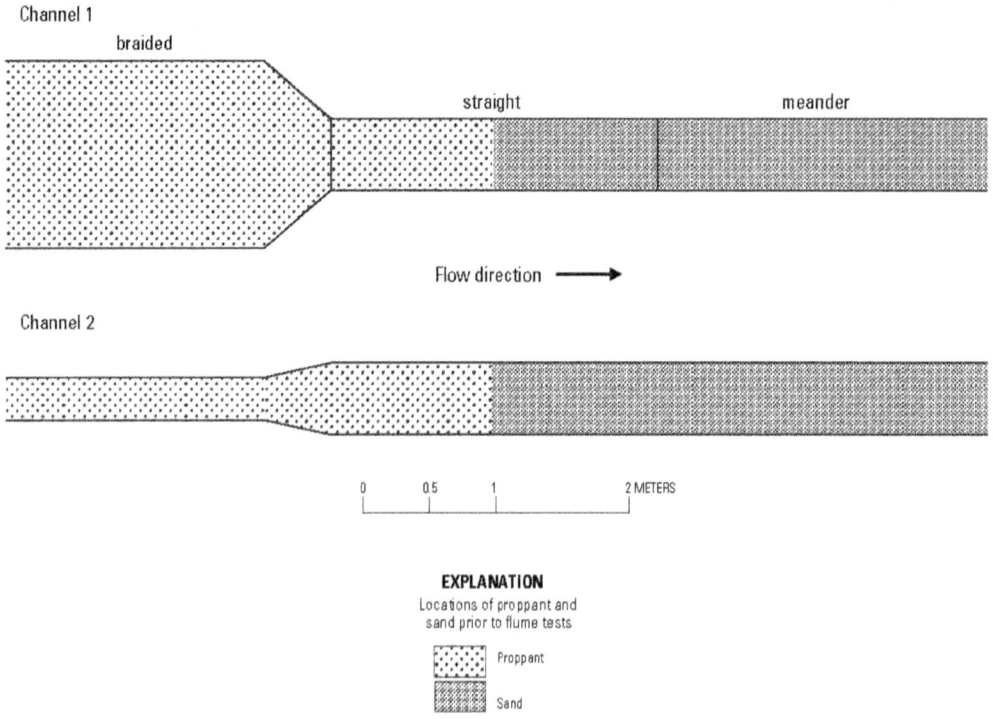

Figure 2–1. Diagram showing configuration of channels 1 and 2.

Table 2–1. Channel characteristics for the braided, straight, and meander reaches of the existing Kootenai River and channel 1 for the corresponding discharges of 500 cubic meters per second and 3.0 liters per second.

[The straight reach in the channel 1 had two slope and D_{50} values. m, meters; W/D, width/depth ratio; D_{50}, median grain-size diameter; cm, centimeters]

Characteristic	Kootenai River			Channel 1		
	Braided	**Straight**	**Meander**	**Braided**	**Straight**	**Meander**
Width (m)	400	200	200	1.20	0.50	0.50
Depth (m)	2	3	6.5	0.0125	0.0225	0.03
W/D	200	67	31	96	22	17
Slope	4.6×10^{-4}	1.7×10^{-4}	2.0×10^{-5}	5.4×10^{-3}	$5.4 \times 10^{-3}/ 0$	0
D_{50} (cm)	3.36	1.67	0.022	0.13	0.13/0.019	0.019

The resulting channel 1 was 1.25 m wide for the upper 2.4 m of the flume (figs. 2–1 and 2–2*A*). The next 0.5-m-long section tapered to a width of 0.5 m, patterned after the transition from the braided reach to the straight and meander reaches, and the remainder of the channel was 0.5 m wide. The bed in the lower one-half of the flume channel was screeded to be 0.005 m lower than that in the upper one-half to approximate the increase in depth between the braided and meander reaches.

Channel 2 was 0.25 m wide in the upper one-third segment and expanded over the next 0.5-m portion to the same width (0.5 m) as channel 1 (figs. 2–1 and 2–2*D*). The bed of the braided reach was screeded to match the meander reach depth. Channel 2, was therefore, narrower and deeper than channel 1 in the reach used to approximate the braided reach of the river. Channel 2 was not explicitly based on the design channel dimensions; nevertheless, this channel allowed us to gain insight about how altering channel geometry influences sediment transport and provided a means to make measurements used to test the modeling approach.

The sediment size, sediment placement, and flume slopes were the same in channels 1 and 2. The sediment used to

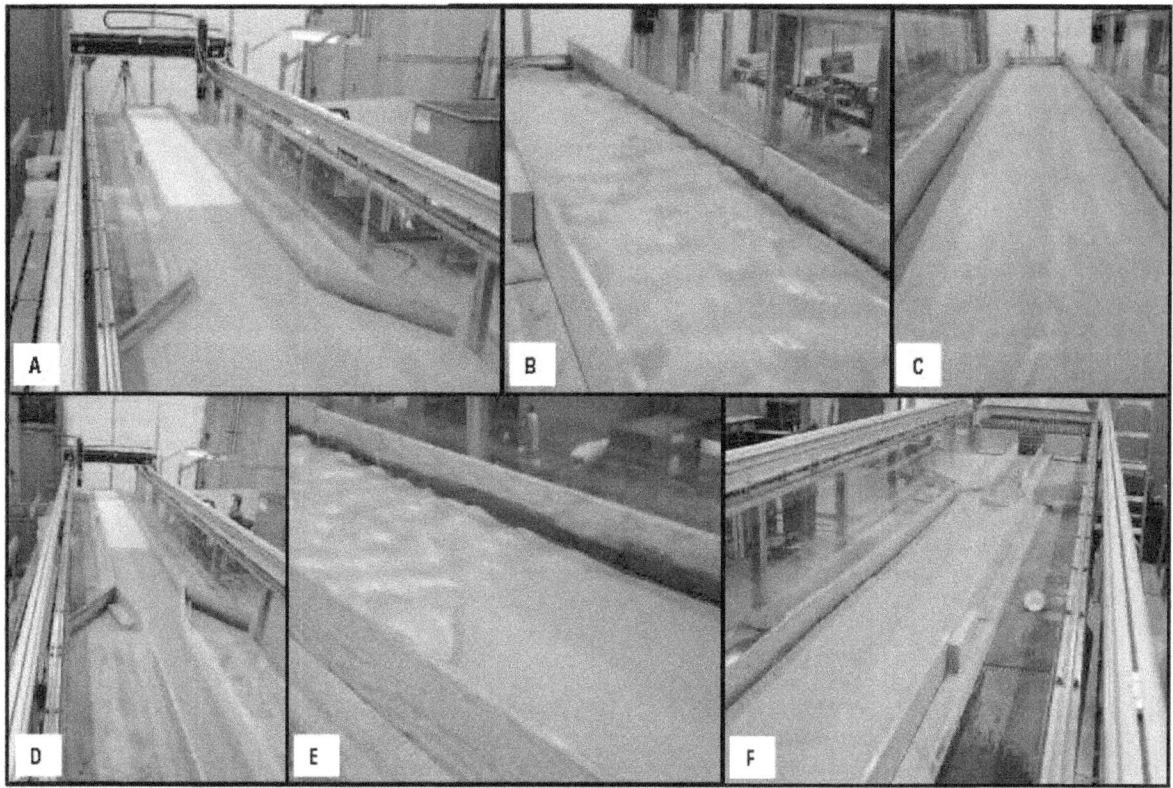

Figure 2–2.   Photograph of flume work showing:
   A. Channel 1 prior to flume experiments
   B. Channel 1 dunes formed during 2.9-liters-per-second experiment
   C. Channel 1 dunes partially washed out and covered by proppant during 11.46-liters-per-second experiment
   D. Channel 2 prior to flume experiments
   E. Channel 2 gravel front and dunes during 3.04-liters-per-second experiment
   F. Channel 2 gravel dune and bed scoured during 11.41-liters-per-second experiment

approximate gravel had a D_{50} of 0.13 cm. The material used was 12/18 micro-hydrofracturing proppant, which is man-made ceramic spheres that have a specific gravity similar to that of sand. Proppant is more uniform in size and roundness than natural grains. The sand used in the meander reach of the channels had a D_{50} of 0.019 cm, which was only slightly finer than the average grain size in the actual meander reach. Fine sand was used in the flume channels because it is difficult to scale down fine sand without using silt or clay, which are more cohesive and have different transport properties than sand. Proppant was used in the upper one-half of each channel and sand was used in the lower one-half. The flume was set to a slope of 0.0054, but the bed in the lower one-half of each channel was screeded to be nearly level to reflect the near zero slope of the meander reach.

Flume Experiments

An initializing experiment was made of channel 1 in order to set the tailgate to the appropriate height for all subsequent model simulations. This experiment was done at a discharge of approximately 3 L/s for about 30 minutes, and the tailgate at the downstream end of the flume was adjusted until the depth of water in the flume matched calculated values (table 2–1) as closely as possible. During this experiment, the proppant initially scoured from two small pits in the transition between the wide and narrow portions of the channel. This material was deposited downstream in the straight reach of the channel. After an initial period of erosion and deposition, there was little to no further transport of material. The fine sand in the lower one-half of the channel formed dunes (fig. 2–2*B*) similarly to the way in which dunes are formed in the meander reach of the Kootenai River. The channel bed was then resurveyed and a discharge of 2.91 L/s was applied without rescreeding the bed. This experiment lasted for 1 hour, during which sediment transport was negligible (fig. 2–3). The water-surface profile for this experiment indicates a hydraulic jump had formed between 3 and 4 m downstream from the top of the channel (fig. 2–4).

The bed of channel 1 was resurveyed and a discharge of 11.46 L/s was applied for approximately 34 minutes without rescreeding the bed. During this experiment there was no transport of proppant in the braided reach, likely because of

backwater conditions that had formed in the transition to the narrower channel. Although a similar process may occur to some extent in the transition between the braided reach and the straight reach in the Kootenai River, the backwater from the transition does not limit transport in the Kootenai River as much as the larger scale backwater from Kootenay Lake. In channel 1, some proppant transport occurred just upstream from the original scour pits, and transport was substantial starting at the upstream end of the straight reach near x-coordinate 4.4 (fig. 2–3). A gravel front formed and migrated the full length of the channel by the end of the experiment. At the end of the experiment, the dunes were partially washed out

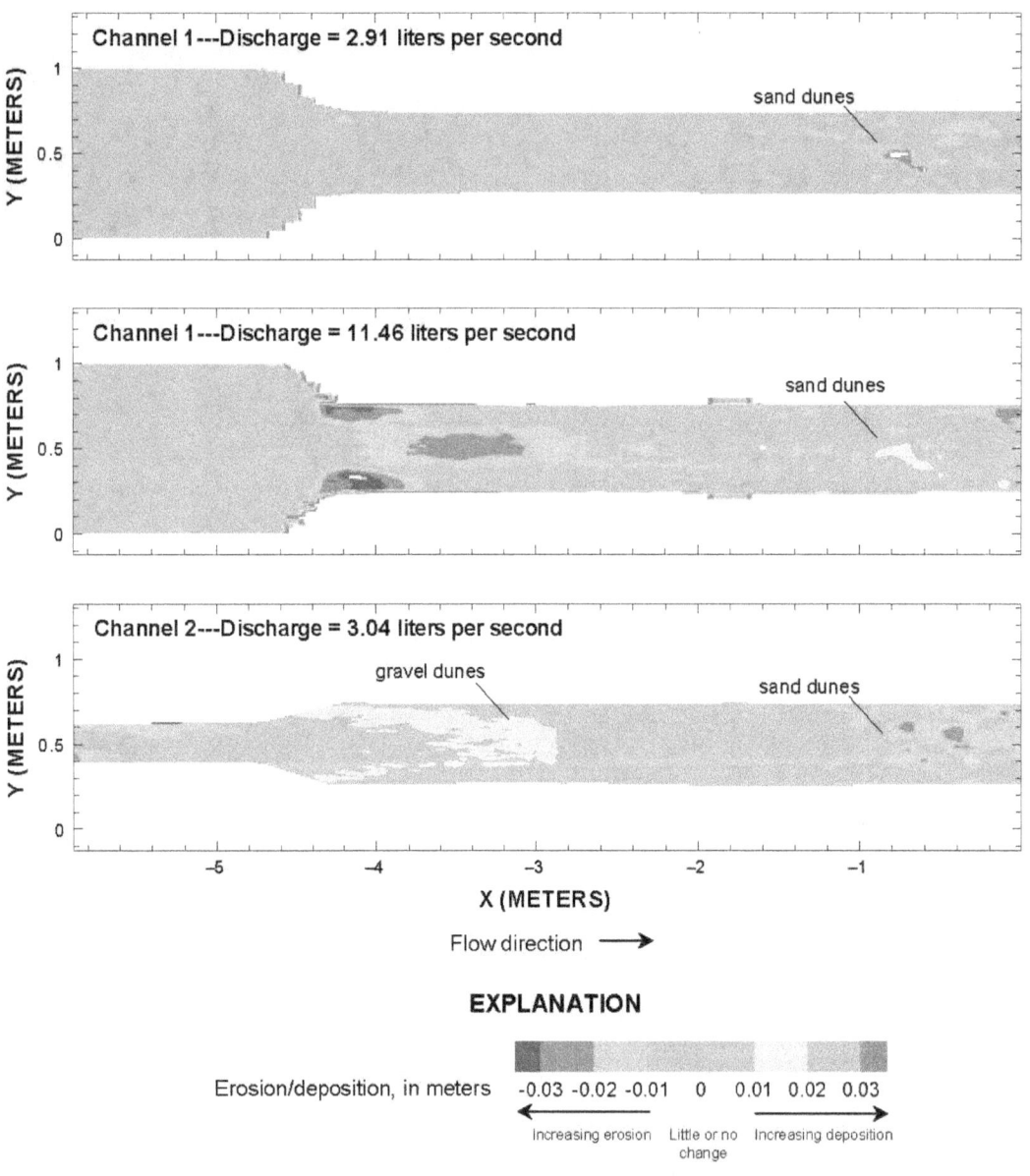

Figure 2–3.   Erosion and deposition for both channel configurations for three flume experiments.

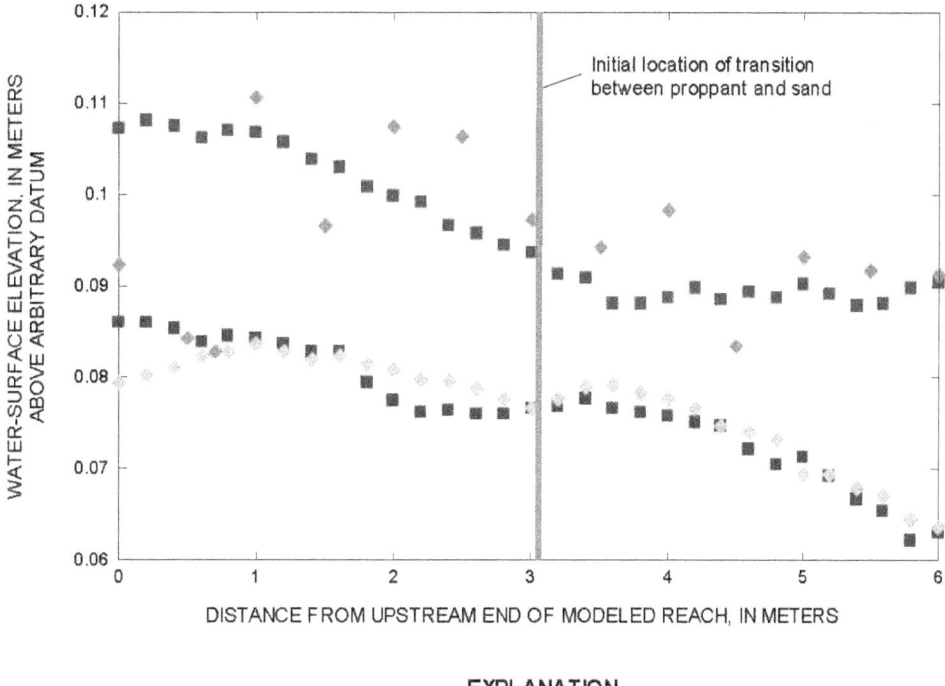

Figure 2–4. Graphs showing measured water-surface profiles for both channel configurations at each discharge.

in the lower reach and covered by gravel, leaving a relatively uniform bed (figs. 2–2C and 2–3). A long pool formed in the straight reach below the scour pits but ended near the original sand/proppant interface. The water-surface profile for this experiment shows an abrupt change in slope between 3 and 4 m from the upstream end of the modeled reach (fig. 2–4).

Channel 2 was then constructed by altering the upper one-third of channel 1 to make it narrower and deeper. This channel was surveyed and a discharge of 3.04 L/s was applied for 1 hour. The narrower configuration at the upstream end of the channel allowed substantial transport of proppant in the upper one-third (braided section) of the channel; proppant quickly scoured down to the bed of the flume in this section. By the end of the experiment, the bed was completely scoured for the first 0.5 m of the channel, and one-half of the bed thickness was scoured for almost another 0.5 m. A gravel front started near the expansion point and traveled downstream approximately 0.23 m into the sand-bedded portion of the channel (figs. 2–2E and 2–3). Two to three less-pronounced gravel dunes followed the main gravel front. A pool formed at the expansion point, and sand dunes developed in the lower one-half of the channel. The water-surface profile for this

discharge was similar to that for the low-discharge experiment in channel 1, except that the hydraulic jump is farther upstream, between 2 and 3 m from the upstream end of the modeled reach (fig. 2–4).

Because substantial sediment was transported in the upper one-half of the channel 2, the proppant material was rescreeded back to the initial conditions before a second experiment was done at the higher discharge. However, the dunes that developed in the lower one-half of the channel during the lower discharge were not altered. The higher discharge of 11.41 L/s was maintained for approximately 30 minutes. Proppant was rapidly scoured from the narrow portion of the flume and created a gravel front that quickly migrated downstream and reached the end of the channel near the end of the experiment (fig. 2–2F). Gravel dunes developed in the 0.5-m-wide portion of the flume. The proppant appeared to be saltating in a 1-cm-thick layer above the bed. At the end of the experiment, proppant had scoured the full width of the bed, from the upstream end of the flume through the expansion point, forming a pool in the first 0.30 m of the 0.5-m-wide reach. The water-surface profile throughout the reach was extremely erratic owing to large and variable surface waves and potentially two or more hydraulic jumps (fig. 2–4). We made measurements of the water-surface profile every 0.5 m, but variations in the measurements were substantial and could not be used for additional analysis.

Modeling Strategy

Generally the topography surveyed at the end of a given discharge experiment was imported into the MD_SWMS and used in the corresponding model simulation (fig. 2–5). This is because the water-surface profiles were measured toward the end of the experiment after the bed had potentially changed substantially from the conditions at the beginning of the experiment. The only exception was channel 1 at the low discharge, which was modeled by using the topography measured before the experiment because little or no transport of sediment occurred during that experiment. The same computational grid was used to model all cases. This grid was 5.85 m long and 1.25 m wide and had 1- by 1-cm-sized grid cells. The grid was fit to the surveyed data in the streamwise direction, which omits the top 0.7 m of the flume. In the cross-stream direction, the generated grid was set to the full width of the flume (1.25 m), which is slightly wider than the surveyed width of 1.0 m. The topography in the upper one-third of the flume was extended to the 1.25-m width by generating additional points at the end of each cross section using the elevations surveyed at the ends of the cross section. All points outside of the channel were set to the same elevation in order to create smooth channel walls.

The measured water-surface profiles were used to calibrate the roughness for each modeled flume case. A constant roughness value was used when possible, but a two-part roughness was required for two modeled cases because bedforms caused roughness to vary longitudinally in the channel. Calibration was determined by visual observation on the basis of varying the roughness of two areas and the location of the boundary between them using drag coefficients calibrated in increments of 0.001 to 0.0001, depending on the sensitivity of the model to minor changes (table 2–2). The root-mean square (RMS) error could not be used to select the final calibrated parameters because the set of parameters that produced the smallest RMS error values did not necessarily produce the best fit to the shape of the measured water-surface profile.

In general the MD_SWMS-simulated water-surface profiles matched the measured flume water-surface profiles quite well. In channel 1, the fit was reasonable except that the sharp transition in the measured water surface at the higher discharge could not be replicated exactly (fig. 2–6). The simulated water-surface profile in the lower one-third of the channel was fairly insensitive to the drag coefficient. The roughness values changed substantially between the high and low discharges. At the lower discharge, the upper portion of the flume was hydraulically smooth compared to the lower reach where large-scale sand dunes developed. At the higher discharge, these dunes were washed out and the interstices

of the overriding proppant were filled with sand, making the lower section hydraulically smoother. In channel 2, the measured water-surface profile was matched reasonably well, except for the upper four points.

Channel 2 had a hydraulic jump near the head gate that caused the water-surface elevations to be artificially low for the first four measured points near the top of the modeled reach at the lower discharge (fig. 2–7). The roughness in the upper portion of channel 2 was similar to the calibrated roughness in channel 1, but the lower portion of the channel was substantially rougher. The model for the highest discharge in channel 2 could not be calibrated because the measured water-surface profile was too irregular.

Analysis of Modeling Results

The following section presents sediment transport results from the simulated flume channel experiments. The model-predicted mobility of proppant and the transport mode of sand are evaluated for each flume scenario. These results are compared to sediment transport observed during the flume experiments, which provides a means of testing the predictive capability of the multidimensional modeling approach.

Mobility of Proppant

Sediment mobility was determined by using a similar process to that described in the main body of this report. The critical shear stress for sediment transport calculated by using the equations in Parker and others (2003) was 0.37 N/m^2 for the proppant and 0.10 N/m^2 for the sand used in the flume experiments. Table 2–3 shows the critical shear stress necessary for initial motion, depending on the critical shear value used. Shear stress maps for each experiment are shown in figure 2–8.

For the higher discharge in channel 1, the shear stress mapped is directly from the MD_SWMS model. However, the dunes that formed in the lower portion of the channel 1 and channel 2 at the lower discharge caused the roughness to increase in this area. Increased roughness causes the total boundary shear stress, τ_b, to increase because τ_b is composed of the sum of the skin friction component, τ_{sf} and a form drag component, τ_{fd}, owing to drag on the dunes so that

$$\tau_b = \tau_{sf} + \tau_{fd} . \qquad (2\text{–}1)$$

In order to calculate the actual stress on the bed of the channel, the form drag on the dunes must be removed. The stress on the bed was calculated by applying a correction to the total stress developed by Nelson and others (1993) such that

$$\tau_{sf} = \frac{\tau_b}{1 + \dfrac{C_d}{2K^2}\dfrac{H_d}{\lambda}\left(1n\dfrac{H_d}{z_0} - 1\right)^2} \qquad (2\text{–}2)$$

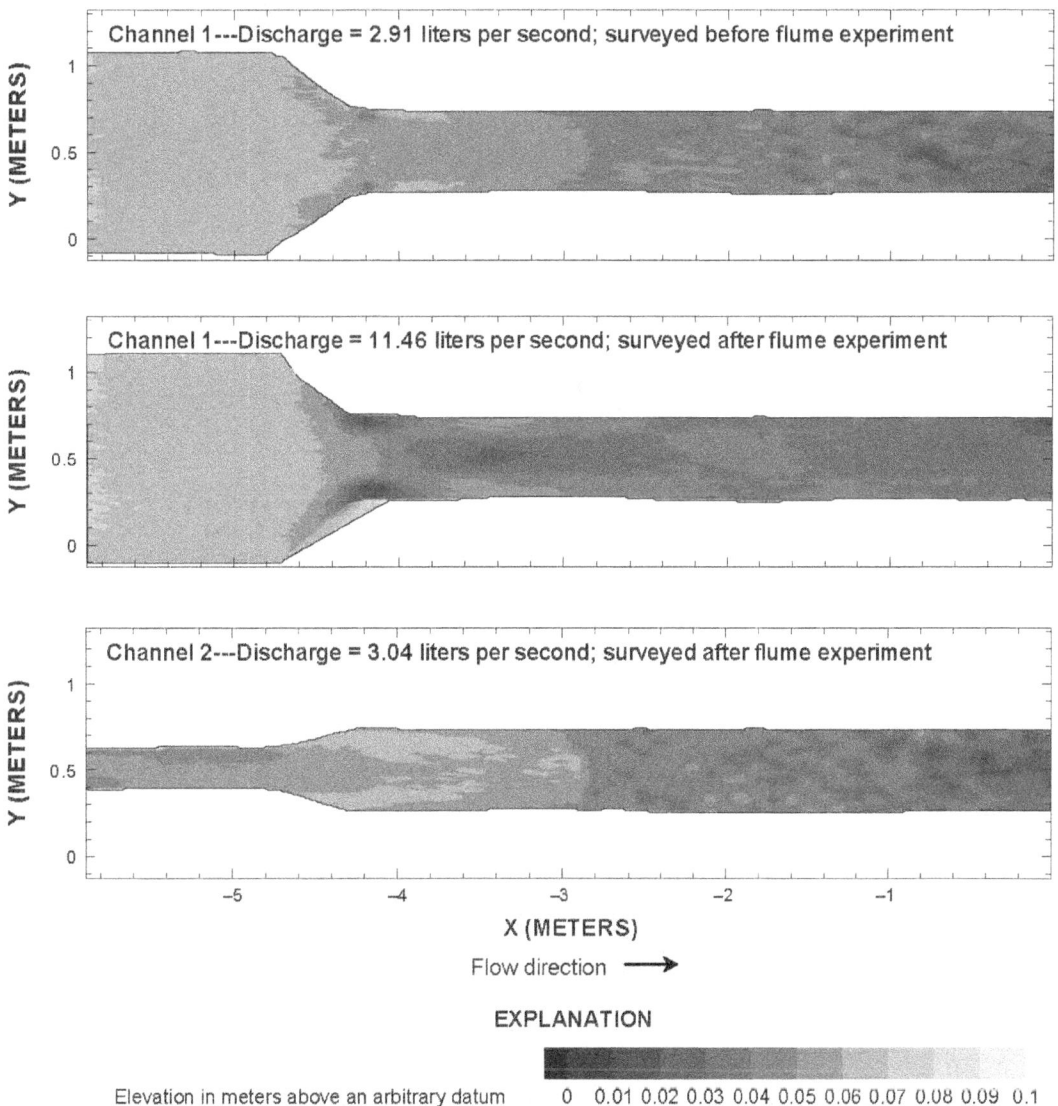

Figure 2–5. Topography for each modeled case.

Table 2–2. Summary calibration data for each simulated case.

[m, meters; L/s, liters per second; m²/s, square meters per second; -, no data; RMS, root-mean square]

Channel	Discharge (L/s)	Downstream boundary (m)	Drag coefficient (dimensionless)	Lateral eddy viscosity (m²/s)	RMS error (m)
1	2.91	0.0629	0.008/0.029	0.000044	0.0012
1	11.46	0.087	0.0025	0.00017	0.0014
2	3.04	0.06353	0.007/0.052	0.000074	0.0024
2	11.41	-	-	-	-

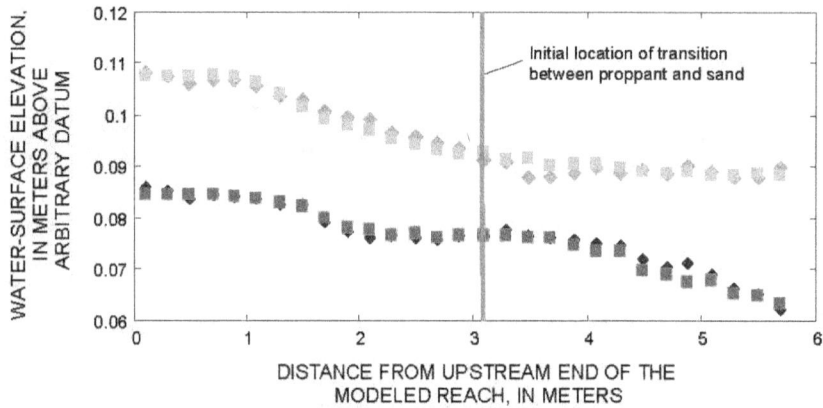

Figure 2–6. Graphs showing measured and simulated water-surface elevations for channel 1.

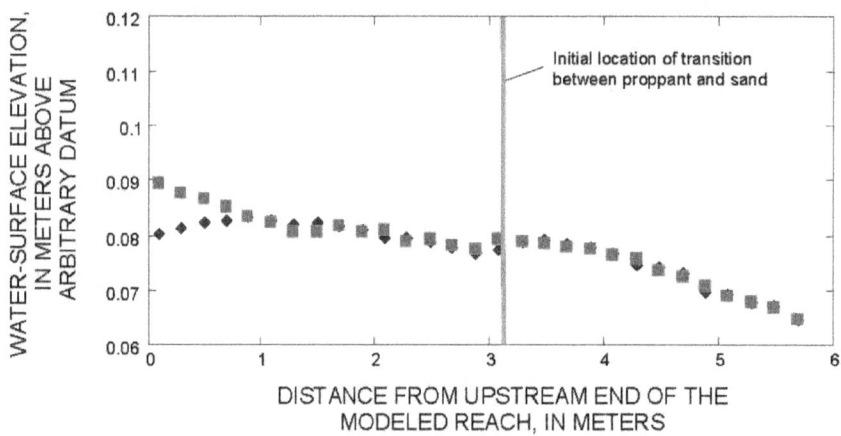

Figure 2–7. Graphs showing measured and simulated water-surface elevations for channel 2.

where C_d is the drag coefficient for dunes taken as 0.2, κ is von Karman's constant (0.408), z_0 is the boundary roughness length taken as 0.1 times the D_{50} of the sand, H_d is the bedform height, and λ is the wavelength of the dunes. The wavelength and dune height were estimated by using the surveyed topography data and the photographs of the bed at the end of the flume experiments. This method was applied in all locations where the calibrated drag coefficient in the lower portion of the flume was greater than the coefficient in the rest of the flume.

Table 2–3. Four different critical dimensionless shear stress values and the resulting critical shear stress values for the D_{50} of the proppant (0.13 cm) and the sand (0.019 cm) used in flume experiments.

[D_{50}, mean sediment grain size diameter; N/m², newtons per square meter]

Critical dimensionless shear stress, τ_{cr}	Critical shear stress τ^* (N/m²)	
	Proppant	Sand
0.018 / 0.032*	0.37	0.10
0.03	0.63	0.09
0.045	0.95	0.14
0.06	1.26	0.18

*values used to evaluate mobility in this report

On the basis of this analysis, the shear stress in channel 1 at the lower discharge is too low to move the proppant in the braided reach until just upstream from the point on the bed where the flow scoured two small pits at the channel-width transition. Shear stress is high enough to move the proppant through all but the edges of the channel from –4.4 m down to about –2.2 m. Downstream from the –2.2-m point, there are only a few small pockets with stress sufficient to mobilize the proppant. The simulated sediment transport is similar to that observed in the flume test in terms of the starting location of initial proppant motion. The location of the small proppant bars in the middle one-third of the channel also coincides with locations where shear stress is below the threshold for motion. In the flume, very little material moved into the sand reach and any that did became trapped in the lee of the sand dunes.

Shear stress in channel 1 at the higher discharge of 11.46 L/s is sufficient to move the proppant from just above the transition in channel width to the end of the flume (–4.4 to 0.0 m). This is consistent with the observed start of proppant transport and the migration of a gravel front to the downstream end of the flume. The location of highest stress near the transition in channel width was also the location of the greatest scour during this experiment.

In channel 2 at the low discharge of 3.04 L/s, the simulated shear stress is sufficient to move the proppant from the top of the reach down to about –2.2 m. This result is supported by observations that substantial transport occurred near the top of the modeled reach, and that a gravel front was formed that moved into the sand reach but not through to the end of the flume.

Transport Mode of Sand

The simulated shear stress is sufficient to move the sand at all locations except along the edges of the channel for all channel configurations and discharges modeled. Given that the sand was capable of motion, the transport mode of the sand was investigated to determine if the model was able to predict the transport mode accurately on the basis of Rouse numbers (fig. 2–9). The shear velocity used in the Rouse number equation needs to be adjusted for the lower portion of the flume that contained dunes at lower discharges. This was done by converting the recalculated stress for equation 2–2 into shear velocity (u_*) by using

$$u_* = \sqrt{\tau_{tf}/\rho} \; , \qquad (2\text{–}3)$$

where ρ is the density of water. Rouse numbers in channel 1 at the higher discharge and in the dune-free portions of the other cases were calculated by using the modeled boundary shear stress.

Overall, the transport mode observed in the flume experiments was captured by the MD_SWMS model. At the lower discharge in the channel 1, Rouse numbers indicate that the sand would move as bedload in the braided portion of the channel, in suspension in the middle one-third of the channel, and as a patchwork of bedload and suspension from about –2.2 m through the end of the channel. These predictions are supported by the presence of dunes in the lower reach. In channel 1 at the discharge of 11.46 L/s, Rouse numbers indicate that the sand would move as bedload in the top of the reach and some fraction would be in suspension throughout the rest of the channel. This is consistent with the partial washout of the dunes at this discharge. In channel 2 at low discharge, Rouse numbers indicate that the sand would move primarily in suspension in the upper one-half of the channel and as a patchwork of bedload and suspended material in the portion of the channel where dunes were formed. This was verified by the formation of dunes in the lower one-half of channel 2.

Considerations for Channel Restoration Design

Observations made during the flume experiments and the efforts to model the flume channels indicate that altering the braided reach has the potential to change sediment transport. By narrowing and deepening channel 2, the braided reach became able to transport the proppant at the lower discharge, when previously channel 1 was unable to move this material. Channel 2 was also able to move the proppant through the straight reach and into the meander reach, whereas channel 1 had negligible transport in these reaches. At the higher discharges, both the channel 1 and the narrower and deeper channel 2 displayed substantial transport of the sediment; however,

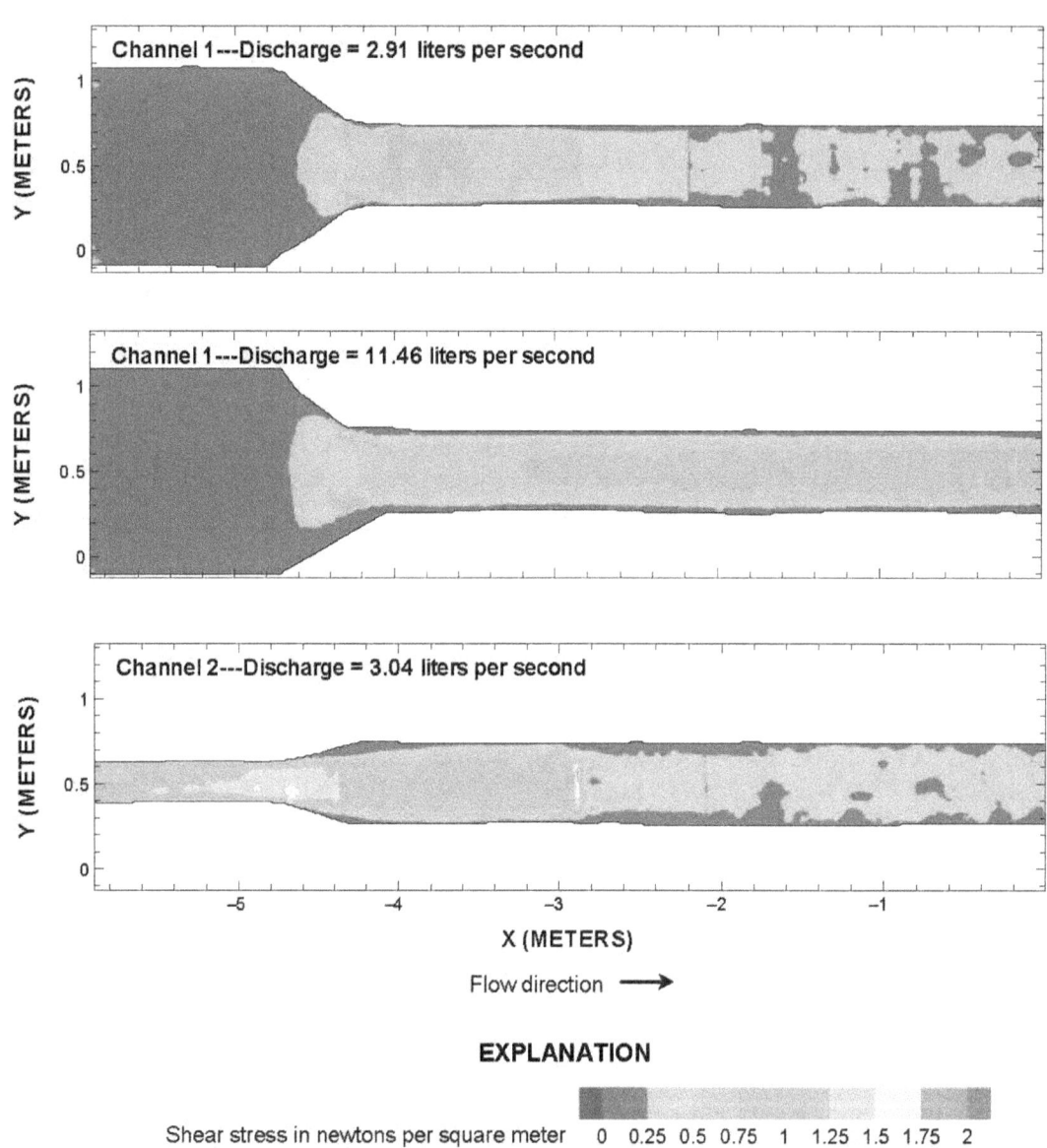

Figure 2–8. Simulated shear stress for channels 1 and 2 at each modeled discharge.

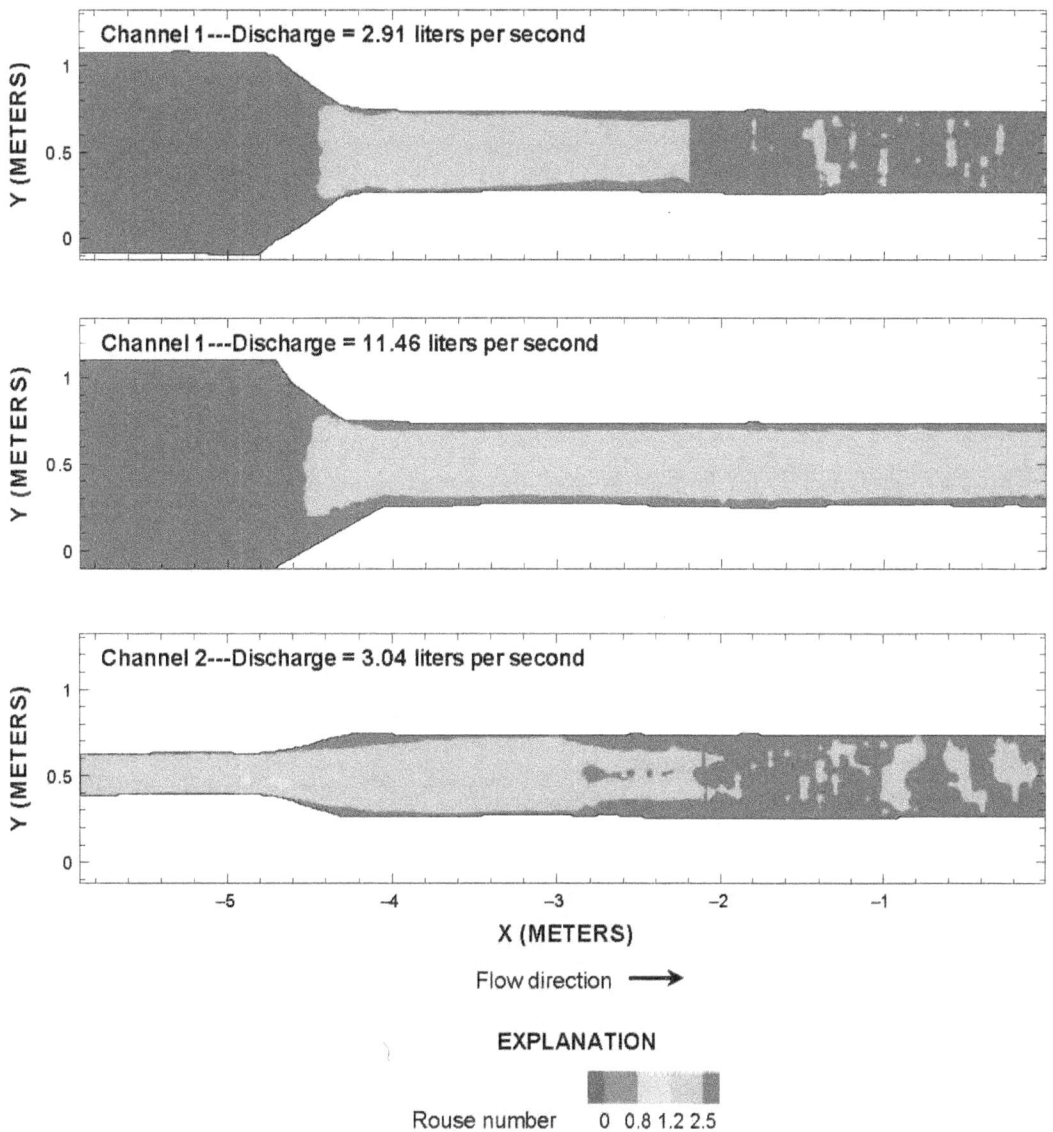

Figure 2–9. Simulated Rouse number for channels 1 and 2 at each modeled discharge.

the bed of channel 2 eroded more rapidly and material was deposited in the meander reach of channel 2.

The flume results cannot be directly applied to what may actually occur for either the existing Kootenai River or any constructed channel owing to a number of simplifications and limitations of flume models in general. Simplifications include the straight channel alignment, uniform channel geometry, lack of mixed grain sizes, and use of a single downstream boundary condition for all discharges. One of the limitations was the flume length, which introduced boundary conditions at the upstream and downstream ends of the channel that are inconsistent with those for the actual channel. Another potential source of error was the proppant material used, which consisted of unusually uniform and round grains that could move more easily than actual sediment of the same nominal diameter.

However, some inferences between the flume experiments and the Kootenai River can be made, although it remains difficult to predict how the design channel will function until it is constructed. If the designed channel is competent at moving the average grain-size sediment through the braided reach, there are a number of considerations and possible outcomes. The first possibility is that very little sediment is delivered into the braided reach. This is essentially the case tested in the flume scenarios because we did not feed sediment into the flume. The proppant transported, therefore, was essentially mined from the channel bed. If a similar process occurred in the design channel, the areas of erosion and the subsequent areas of deposition downstream could affect the form and function of the channel. This could also cause the bed of the river to coarsen over time, as the more easily moved grain sizes are transported out of the system. If however, substantial amounts of sediment are delivered to the braided reach, erosion in the reach would not be a factor. But, even if gravel can be transported through the braided reach, rather than depositing in the reach, the material would be deposited

in downstream reaches, which could alter channel morphology and function in those areas. This highlights the importance of measuring bedload transport in the Kootenai River over a range of flow conditions to better characterize sediment delivery and transport for use in the design process. A sediment sampling program has been initiated on the Kootenai River for this purpose (Fosness and Williams, 2009)

Summary and Conclusions

The predictive capability of multidimensional modeling was tested using flume studies of a channel that was loosely patterned after the existing Kootenai River and a second channel designed to simulate narrowing and deepening of the upper portion of the channel. Discharges of approximately 3 L/s and 12 L/s were used in each flume channel to consider the effects of moderate and high flows. Measurements of the channel topography and water-surface profiles in the flume were used to develop and calibrate multidimensional flow models of channel 1 at both discharges and channel 2 at the lower discharge. Patterns of erosion and deposition as well as transport mode observed in the flume were consistent with model simulation results of sediment mobility and transport mode. At lower discharges, sediment mobility and sediment transport were greater in the narrower and deeper channel 2 than in channel 1. The increased transport resulted in scour of the bed in the braided portion of the flume; however, there was no sediment input, which may not be the case in the Kootenai River. Although the flume studies cannot be directly applied to the actual Kootenai River owing to simplifications and scaling related issues, this work demonstrates that flume scenarios can be successfully simulated by using a multidimensional flow model and that this methodology can identify potential design problems or issues that need further consideration.